negative employee attitudes into positive ones and shows how to maintain them. Other effective techniques are also highlighted, such as how to gain and effectively use managerial power.

"Much of management literature is either technology or theory oriented. One is told 'how to'—but not why, when and what else to do if. . . . Or, one is told what 'one could and ought to become'—but not how. Beck and Hillmar put the two together. They offer a lengthy list of solid, practical management techniques in the context of a management theory which recognizes the complexity of the management task. The book is structured around the tri-focus of managing an organization, managing individuals and teams, and managing one's self"—*John C. Bryan, President, Bryan * Weir Associates.*

THE AUTHORS

ARTHUR C. BECK and ELLIS D. HILLMAR are associate professors of organization development at the University of Richmond. They have put their ideas into practice by consulting for numerous firms including IBM, General Electric, Philip Morris, and Digital Equipment Company. They are also co-authors of *Making MBO/R Work.*

Positive Management Practices

*Bringing Out the Best
in Organizations and People*

Arthur C. Beck

Ellis D. Hillmar

Foreword by William Clarkson

Positive
Management Practices

J o s s e y - B a s s   P u b l i s h e r s

San Francisco • London • 1986

106681

POSITIVE MANAGEMENT PRACTICES
Bringing Out the Best in Organizations and People
by Arthur C. Beck and Ellis D. Hillmar

Copyright © 1986 by: Jossey-Bass Inc., Publishers
433 California Street
San Francisco, California 94104
&
Jossey-Bass Limited
28 Banner Street
London EC1Y 8QE

Library of Congress Cataloging-in-Publication Data

Beck, Arthur C.
    Positive management practices.

    (The Jossey-Bass management series)
    Bibliography: p. 223
    Includes index.
    1. Organizational change. 2. Organizational effectiveness. 3. Management. I. Hillmar, Ellis D.
II. Title. III. Series.
HD58.8.B38   1985   658   85-24038
ISBN 0-87589-672-3

Quotations in the Introduction from Joseph A. Alutto's unpublished letter of nomination for the Phillips Award, School of Management, State University of New York at Buffalo, 1978. Used by permission.

Selections in Chapters One and Five adapted from "Managing for Today and Tomorrow," an address presented at Ecology of Work Conference, Pittsburgh, Pa., June 1982, by William Clarkson. Used by permission.

Sections of Chapter Four adapted by permission of the publisher from "Bad Vibes in the Workplace . . . What Managers Can Do to Turn Around Negative Attitudes in an Organization," by Arthur C. Beck and Ellis D. Hillmar, *Management Review*, January 1984 © 1984 AMA Membership Publications Division, American Management Associations, New York. All rights reserved.

The centering exercise in Chapter Thirteen is adapted from *The Centering Book* by Gay Hendricks and Russel Wills © 1975 by Prentice-Hall, Inc. Published by Prentice-Hall, Inc., Englewood Cliffs, NJ 07632. Used by permission.

Figures 1 and 2, Table 1, and portions of the text are taken from A. C. Beck and E. D. Hillmar, *Making MBO/R Work*, © 1976, Addison-Wesley, Reading, Massachusetts, and are used by permission of the publisher. Figure 2 and Table 1 are also used by permission of their originator, John C. Talbot, 14 Canoe Brook Place, Summit, New Jersey, 07901.

Manufactured in the United States of America

JACKET DESIGN BY WILLI BAUM

FIRST EDITION: *First printing, February 1986; Second printing, October 1986*

Code 8602

The Jossey-Bass
Management Series

Foreword

Why is it important for managers and leaders of organizations to read and study this book? The reasons are both global and local, macro and micro, broad-ranging and personal. Managers are told, from every direction, that most national economies, including ours, are moving toward a single world market. However, those of us in industry and government seem to have major difficulty facing this reality of globalization. Thus, we are slow in developing solutions to this relatively new and serious industrial problem of competing in a global market.

The proposed solutions to this problem encompass many facets, ranging from our domestic economy, budgets, and trade deficits and the problems of debtor nations, to the way in which we manage and lead our organizations. Four aspects of these proposed solutions have a relationship to this unusual book:

- For the United States to preserve even its present international competitive position, U.S. industry will have to improve its performance very quickly.
- People are the only true resource of a country and an organization.
- Thoughtful and planned actions concerned with the human

aspect of improving organizational productivity have been conspicuously absent.

- In the view of many people, we need a new national strategy representing a consensus between management, labor, and government.

In their preface, Arthur C. Beck and Ellis D. Hillmar touch on the theme that unites these aspects: ". . . managers frequently want to improve their behavior to become more productive." *Positive Management Practices* is a book for managers who want to improve their own managerial skills and competencies. But it is also much more than this. It is a practical and detailed manual on how to develop a high-involvement organization, one striving for the participation and commitment of its people along with a healthy quality of work life. I consider myself part of the humanistic tradition, with a managerial approach that focuses on people as interdependent and desirous of making commitments to their organizations as a result of involvement and participation. (My perspective is that of a management practitioner with more than thirty-five years in both the private and government sectors—twenty years in various corporate managerial roles, thirteen years as chief executive officer of a multinational manufacturing business that grew to $100 million in sales, and two years as the number two person in a New York state government agency.)

To the extent that there is agreement concerning the precarious competitive condition of U.S. industry, there seems to be a developing view that today's managers need to shift from being coercive, authoritarian order-givers ("I'm not arguing with you, I'm telling you") to empowering, authoritative leader-facilitators ("I care about you; I ask you to participate and develop a commitment to accomplish the vision that we have for this organization"). This book, if properly studied and used, can help leaders and managers develop the skills to become effective practitioners of the type of management that will enable U.S. industry to use its human resources more effectively and competitively. These skills will also be required to build the needed consensus between government and industry.

This concise book discusses and clarifies the tasks that need to be undertaken and the issues that need to be addressed if we are to realize the full potential of the human resources of many organizations:

- values identification
- vision development
- commitment building
- confrontation of people
- empowerment of others
- creativity releasing
- teamwork development
- stress management
- performance reviews

Not only are these subjects discussed, but clear directions are given on how to accomplish them. If we are going to radically improve our management of human resources, we believe that these new skills and behaviors need to be learned and practiced.

Getting any job done involves both a task and a process. The tradition that U.S. managers have inherited from the unparalleled industrial growth of the nineteenth and twentieth centuries is that of being tremendous task accomplishers who show a minimum of concern, if any, for the process involved. If we are going to attain the improved productivity that comes from high-involvement organizations, we need to get these two activities in balance. This is one of the few books that shows the way to achieve this balance. For example, consider the key issue of evaluating individual performance. This is encompassed by responsibility profiles (job descriptions), objectives, performance measurements, evaluations, and performance reviews. Beck and Hillmar point out the inadequacies in many current performance evaluation approaches and then describe how to conduct a more effective evaluation, cognitively, emotionally, and practically, paying attention to both the task and the process.

It is very unusual for one book to contain so much of value for the concerned and aware leader and manager. This is what makes it so significant. And as important, it makes a major contribution to the search for an answer to Charles Dabney's (former president of the University of Cincinnati) challenge to all organizations: "The important question to be asked about every human institution is, 'What is it doing for the making of better men and women?' "

Buffalo, New York   William Clarkson
December 1985   President, Chief Executive Officer,
                                and Chairman of Graphic Controls
                                Corporation (1970-1983)

                                Executive Deputy Commissioner,
                                Department of Commerce,
                                State of New York (1983-1985)

Preface

Many managers have had considerable management training and have a good knowledge of sound management practices. But they often fail to apply this knowledge to their day-to-day activities. We believe that managers frequently want to improve their behavior to become more productive. However, they often do not know how to make these improvements or are unaware that they are stopping themselves from changing their behavior. Barriers to change may include a poor concept of self-worth, fear, hostility, anxiety, resentment, or guilt. Individuals may have no real experience with the new behavior they want and they may find little or no support for managing in a new way.

Positive Management Practices: Bringing Out the Best in Organizations and People provides options for managers who want to change and to improve their managerial capabilities. This book brings together practices from management, organization development, and personality theory with an emphasis on implementation. Increasingly, today's managers must be able to adopt techniques from all three of these areas to be most effective. Managers seem to achieve the most productive response when their units are actively contributing to the success of the organization and when they and their subordinates are achieving their own goals as well as those of the organization as a whole. Managers must be clear about what is expected and must talk about tasks, behavior, and specific performance expectations in a positive and supportive way.

Positive Management Practices fills a void in the management literature. Most management books focus on managerial and organizational concepts and say little about the personal qualities of successful managers. Most descriptions of the success of the Marriott Corporation, for example, stress their goals, objectives, and vision. But before *In Search of Excellence,* little was said about the late J. W. Marriott, Sr.'s, attention to details, such as reading every complaint from customers. Also infrequently mentioned was the catering manager's description of being invited to lunch with Marriott himself. For the catering manager, this experience was a highlight of his career. Although immeasurable, the impact of such managerial practices is extremely important at the personal performance level.

Today's managers need new skills and competencies to improve their performance in a society where major changes are occurring at an increasingly rapid rate. Laws and court decisions on the employment, compensation, promotion, and discipline of minorities, women, the aged, and people with handicaps strongly influence what a manager can and cannot do without being sued. Technological changes can make successful products obsolete in a short period of time. Deregulation, divestiture, and mergers can change a safe, secure environment into an unstable and insecure one in a matter of weeks. Managers need to feel positive about themselves and others and confident that they can handle any problems facing them, even the dissolution of their job or unit. This book will give managers the tools and techniques to manage their own stress, fears, and concerns and to help others manage theirs.

Overview of the Contents

We define positive management practices as those actions that produce positive results for the organization in both the short and the long term. Negative practices may yield short-term "results," but the total situation will probably deteriorate in the long run. Positive results that contribute to the mission of the organization are important for increased productivity. In a positive environment, there is a much greater likelihood of individual commitment to the success of the organization. Individuals will be motivated to do everything in their power to accomplish their own goals. This will be reflected not only in the bottom line but also in satisfied customers or clients, lower turnover and absenteeism, fewer accidents and grievances, and in confident handling of crises and unexpected changes.

We wrote this book to make managers more aware of the benefits available from managing in a way that develops positive attitudes and behavior. Managers, supervisors, and individual employees will find many tools and techniques designed to help them achieve positive results by changing their way of managing and relating. Descriptions and examples illustrate various options and their results.

Positive Management Practices is divided into three parts with an Introduction and Conclusion. The Introduction clarifies what we mean by positive practices and why they work. This chapter also provides the reader with a "road map" for the journey through the book.

Part One consists of five chapters that examine the practices that establish the direction and climate for the whole organization. Chapter One provides an explanation of the importance of values, both personal and organizational, and their influence on behavior. We discuss ways of identifying value differences, evaluating the significance of these differences, and using these differences for the benefit of the organization, and we analyze why acceptance of these value differences is vital to positive practices.

Chapter Two focuses on ways of recognizing and articulating organization results and examines why they form a key element in the implementation of positive practices. We then describe the process of setting goals and achieving commitment through a results-oriented management system and propose ways of developing managerial vision as a focusing and integrating tool.

The achievement of organization results depends on individuals knowing what is expected of them. Chapter Three explores the different ways of clarifying roles and responsibilities. When people clearly understand what is expected of them and how their efforts contribute to the success of the organization, commitment and motivation are most likely to follow.

The value of positive energy is the subject of Chapter Four. In addition, we suggest eight ways of changing negative attitudes to positive ones while maintaining a high level of positive energy in the work environment.

Chapter Five, the final chapter in Part One, deals with cultural norms. This chapter will assist managers in deciding whether the norms in their organization help or hinder positive management practices. Ways of changing those that are hindrances to achieving the desired positive environment are presented.

The five chapters in Part Two describe positive practices that can be useful in managing teams and individuals. Chapter Six leads off with the topic of managing accountability. Being able to hold people accountable and yet be supportive at the same time is critical to successfully managing human resources. And managers must also be accountable to their employees. Accountability is an important factor in improving performance and enhancing feelings of self-worth.

To develop accountability, it is necessary to be willing and able to confront employees in a caring, supportive, and yet tough-minded manner. How a manager can accomplish this is discussed in Chapter Seven. This chapter examines the need for preparation before a confrontation and for maintaining one's own positive attitude, explores ways of handling personal feelings and internal barriers effectively, and offers suggestions on how to actually carry out the confrontation.

Chapter Eight discusses the use and importance of empowerment. The effective harnassing of the power of individual employees has important applications to such areas as creativity. This chapter explores the ways in which managers can empower themselves while encouraging others to use their power also.

The means of identifying and removing barriers to the full use of people's creative powers are covered in Chapter Nine. In addition, this chapter explores ways of creating and maintaining a positive environment that fosters creative thinking by individuals and teams.

Chapter Ten examines teamwork and the ways of encouraging people to think and work interdependently with each other and with other units in the organization to accomplish the mission.

Part Three is devoted to the manager as a person. Chapter Eleven discusses the tactics for overcoming internal barriers that prevent us from doing what we want to do and are capable of doing. These tactics will help both managers and their subordinates deal with their fear, anger, guilt, and anxiety so they can accept themselves and achieve a strong sense of self-worth.

Constructive and supportive approaches to managing stress are described in Chapter Twelve. This chapter also outlines a holistic stress-management program that integrates the physical, psychological, and spiritual aspects of being.

Chapter Thirteen presents specific techniques for meditation, affirmations, and visualization. These techniques are useful for managing stress, accomplishing goals, and achieving desired changes.

The Conclusion offers guidelines for getting started in a positive direction and for implementing the tools and techniques described in this book. The positive results that can be expected, as well as some expected barriers to change that may be encountered, are offered as guides for managers who wish to develop their positive practices.

Acknowledgments

During the last twenty years we have been fortunate to have worked with many of the consultants who have provided leadership in the areas of management by objectives and organization development. These were formative years in these fields, and we grew with them and contributed to their integration. Similarly, various authorities in the fields of Gestalt psychology, transactional analysis, neurolinguistic programming, values clarification, visualization techniques, spirituality, family therapy, and Jungian psychology have helped us to integrate these concepts into management and organization theory. The imprint of these sources is contained in this book, and we acknowledge with appreciation all those who have contributed to our growth and understanding.

We appreciate the support of Richard J. Dunsing, director of the Institute for Business and Community Development of the University of Richmond, and of the staff members of the institute. Their concern and encouragement along the way have been very supportive.

We are indebted to William Clarkson of Graphic Controls for providing us with a living model of a chief executive officer who applied most of these concepts both effectively and profitably. His willingness to share his understanding of that experience is noteworthy.

Our publisher has been most helpful in giving us meaningful feedback on our manuscript. Most of all we appreciate the untiring efforts of Larry Davis, our editorial adviser, who supported us through the review process and helped us integrate a wide variety of comments.

The assistance we received from Donna Hillmar, who handled the word processing of this manuscript, was invaluable.

Finally, we thank our many clients and seminar participants who have shared with us in developing and integrating the practices presented in this book while learning to apply them to their own organizations.

Richmond, Virginia   Arthur C. Beck
December 1985   Ellis D. Hillmar

Contents

The Authors

Arthur C. Beck is an associate professor of organization development in the Institute for Business and Community Development of the University of Richmond in Richmond, Virginia. He holds a B.S. degree in business administration from the University of Richmond (1940) and an M.B.A. degree from the University of Pennsylvania (1941).

Beck is a member of the American Society for Training and Development, the Association of Humanistic Psychology, the Association for Creative Change, and trustee emeritus of the Management by Objectives Institute. He has coauthored two books with Ellis D. Hillmar: *Making MBO/R Work* (1976) and *A Practical Approach to Organization Development through MBO—Selected Readings* (1972). He has also authored or coauthored numerous other articles on management by objectives, organization development, productivity, management development, performance appraisal, and church management. He is a consultant to many organizations in the areas of business, industry, government, health care, education, and religion. He is a member of the editorial board and has served as guest editor of the *Journal of Religion and the Applied Behavioral Sciences*.

Ellis D. Hillmar is an associate professor of organization development in the Institute for Business and Community Development of the University of Richmond in Richmond, Virginia. He has a B.A. degree in music education from the University of Colorado (1952) and an M.S. degree in business from the University of Colorado (1962).

Hillmar is a member of the Organization Development Network and the Richmond chapter of the American Society for Training and Development. With Arthur C. Beck he has co-authored the two books mentioned earlier, and he has written several articles on management by objectives, organization development, and performance appraisal. He consults with businesses and governmental organizations on implementation issues in various aspects of organization development and performance management through goal setting.

Positive
Management Practices

*Bringing Out the Best
in Organizations and People*

❧❧ Introduction ❧❧

Positive Practices –
What They Are
and Why They Work

❧❧ ❧❧ ❧❧ ❧❧ ❧❧ ❧❧ ❧❧ ❧❧

In some organizations, the atmosphere is heavy with uncertainty, passivity, fear, and even hostility. There is a certain quietness, a sullenness, and people seem to resent interruptions. If people are together, they are behind closed doors. One does not feel welcome in organizations with such negative environments—there are frowns or scowls instead of smiles, and there is little joy present. One gets the sense that people are not enjoying their work and would rather be somewhere else.

In contrast, there is an excitement to organizations with positive environments. Small groups talk intensely in the halls, at the water fountain, and in offices. People are busy but always ready to respond to others. One is greeted with welcoming smiles; there is laughter and a sense that people enjoy being there and are committed to their work. As one manager said, "People's faces even look different in those places. There is joy present. People are caring."

In our work over the past decade helping a variety of organizations and management groups to implement management by objectives for results (MBO/R) and organization develop-

1

ment (OD), we became aware of a significantly higher success rate in organizations where a positive attitude, philosophy, and belief system were present. Thus, we have evolved an approach that involves the use of techniques that encourage managers to develop a positive environment. The positive practices in this book will help the manager to change attitudes, beliefs, and philosophy from negative to positive—or, as some of today's managers see their job, to create an environment in which good people can work.

Where the positive exists, people are receptive to any ideas that will improve their effectiveness. They are always looking for a better way to get the job done. They are confident that they can handle problems and cope with changes. In the negative environment, there is resistance to change and a feeling that things will not improve. One hears such comments as "What's the use?", "Things will never change," "It's their fault." Or there may be smugness: "We are the best and have no need to get better." When this occurs, growth and development stop.

Many managers are finding that the old way of doing things is not working today. Major changes caused by deregulation, legislation, court decisions, international monetary exchange, increased foreign competition, high energy costs, and different values and expectations of workers require new skills and behavior by managers. This has necessitated reductions in force, especially at the middle-management level. Managers are being expected to manage in ways different from those they have used in the past. It is difficult for a manager to change from a style that has been successful and acceptable for years.

The purpose of this book is to provide managers with tools and techniques for creating an environment in which people can perform at their fullest capacity. It is written for managers who wish to improve their skills in managing people, who have the attitude that there is always something that they can do better for their own growth. Our desire is to help these managers attain a balance between a highly productive organization and achieving individuals. While these factors are often seen as opposites, an either/or condition, we see them as both/and. The goal is to be human and productive at the same time—being sensitive to and supportive of others while being tough-minded and holding others accountable. It is the development of relationships and an environment that are high in trust.

This book is unique in that it is concerned with both the human side of managers and the productive side of organizations, an integration of personality theory with organization and management theory. In the "how to" approach, it presents tools and techniques for managers—options for how they can behave differently in difficult situations.

Definition

Positive practices are the things that a person does to produce positive organization results in both the short and long term, with a commitment to the overall success of the company in the long run. This is different from the philosophy of maximizing profit during the current year without regard for the future. Unfortunately, the rewards system in some organizations is based on annual profits, without balancing them with planning, strategic thinking, and profits for the future years. An automobile manufacturing executive has commented that none of his managers think past one year.

Managers who use positive practices are hopeful, helpful, powerful, aware of possibilities and choices, and willing to change. They have both a sense of self-worth and a high regard for their employees as human beings, doing things that will build their self-esteem and increase their ability to get the job done well. The result is that individuals can reach their personal goals while achieving for the organization. We believe that McGregor (1960) was talking about positive practices in his description of managers with Theory Y assumptions about people. Theory Y assumptions are that work is as natural as play and rest and that direction is not the only way to get people to do things, since people are creative and responsible and will exert self-control in the accomplishment of objectives to which they are committed. Managers with Theory Y assumptions are flexible in being able to give direction where needed and participation where appropriate. In contrast, Theory X assumptions are that people work only for security reasons, must be directed and coerced in order to be productive, and are irresponsible, with the result that everyone is supervised in an autocratic manner. The self-fulfilling prophecy works here. If employees are managed with Theory Y assumptions, they are more likely to exhibit positive behavior; if managed with Theory X assumptions, they will most likely behave to match those assumptions. Unfortunately, many managers have seen Theory Y only as permissive and participative.

An example of how positive practices turned a group of unsatisfactory performers into top performers occurred recently at a research laboratory. One project leader had an idea he wanted to research. He received management's approval and asked for a team of five technicians. He was given five people with the technical skills he needed, but they were all unsatisfactory or marginal performers. Using a positive approach, this manager had one of the top performing teams in the laboratory within six months. Comments from the team members included "For the first time I know what is expected of me"; "I know how I am contributing to the goals of my group"; "It was fun when the boss brought in consultants in pertinent subject areas to work with us"; and "It was the first time I had any training to improve my knowledge and skills." This was a very satisfying experience for the project manager.

Advantages

Positive attitudes and a positive environment, in addition to being good for the bottom line, are helpful to managers who are faced with changes that affect their organization. Technological developments can make a company's products obsolete in a short span of time, as has occurred with calculators, watches, printing, and computers. A publisher with whom we are familiar went from leadership in his field to bankruptcy because he would not change his format and method of printing. He resisted suggested changes because, in his mind, his old way had been successful and somehow would bring him success again.

Even though losses were increasing and salespeople were reporting that advertisers wanted something different from what he was offering, he tenaciously held onto the old way. The atmosphere in this organization was highly negative, with much complaining, a sense of futility, blaming, and no motivation to improve. This created so much stress that a number of employees suffered health problems and some even developed alcoholism. Needless to say, he went out of business.

This publisher, who was a very insecure person, could possibly have saved his company by listening to his salespeople, circulation people, and editor. He could have encouraged risk taking and innovation instead of discouraging it. He could have encouraged his people to communicate with each other and with him rather than dominating all conversations and meetings himself. He needed to be able to have people disagree with him without being punished. He could have handled confrontation in a more supportive way, and he needed to accept and encourage confrontation from others.

Positive practices can also reduce turnover and absenteeism. The health of employees will be better as they manage their stress effectively. There will be a higher level of motivation and commitment to the purpose of the organization. People's energies will be channeled into creative thinking to improve themselves and their productivity. There will be emphasis on developing people. Managers will be managing the human resources more effectively. They will be more sensitive to others' needs and more cooperative in accomplishing results for the organization. Conflict will be accepted as normal and dealt with openly, with confidence that it will be resolved. Communication will be straight and honest. There will be trust and caring. Managers will know what is expected of them and be clear with their subordinates about what constitutes satisfactory job performance. Evaluation will be ongoing; accountability and support will be managed. Everyone will know how their job contributes to accomplishing the mission of the organization. They will receive regular feedback, both positive and negative, on their performance.

A good example of an organization that has a positive en-

vironment is Graphic Controls of Buffalo, New York, chosen
for the Phillips Award for quality of work life in 1979. This
organization was described by Alutto (1978, pp. 1-3) as follows:

> I should like to emphasize here that Graphic
> has not only (1) enunciated a humanistic and par-
> ticipative management philosophy and (2) imple-
> mented that philosophy through formal policies
> and informal practices, but also (3) systematically
> studied major areas of employee concern and the
> impact of its policies over time, and (4) made the
> results of this research available both to manage-
> ment personnel and to employees, stockholders and
> the general public. This comprehensive approach
> to management-employee relations is certainly un-
> usual; and the open publication of evaluative re-
> search results is, to the best of our knowledge,
> unique among American companies at this time.
>   Graphic's management philosophy is re-
> flected both in the general atmosphere of its work
> environment and in formal policies. Both produc-
> tion facilities and clerical-managerial areas are lo-
> cated throughout the building. Common use of
> building entrances and elevator banks creates con-
> tinuous opportunity for informal contact among
> persons at all employment levels. Consequently,
> most members of the permanent work force, in-
> cluding the executive officers, are acquainted on a
> first name basis. The only reserved spaces in the
> parking lot are for handicapped employees; and the
> private dining room in the new company cafeteria
> is available for any group or committee meeting,
> not reserved for the executive staff.
>   The single most unusual employment policy
> of the company is the "Weekly Salary Plan," which
> provides virtually unlimited financial security for
> all regular employees unable to work because of ill-
> ness, accident or personal emergency. Other spe-

cific policies include: (1) open job posting, which has been used for many years and which includes a grievance procedure for any responding employee who does not receive adequate consideration; (2) a variety of work-time policies, including flex-time in one unit and in some individual instances, plus opportunities for steady shift assignment as well as rotating shifts; (3) quarterly employee meetings within divisions, providing opportunity for division performance reports and open question-answer sessions with division chiefs; (4) a program of supervisory training available to all employees above the operative level and staffed by University faculty members; (5) tuition assistance for external programs (both vocational and academic) for regular employees at all levels; and (6) a regular program of testing and counseling—personal and career—through the Human Resources Staff which is augmented by a consulting psychologist.

This is a good example of positive practices in action. William Clarkson, the chief executive officer, is a great believer in positive management and results management. These practices paid off for Graphic Controls in lower absenteeism, lower turnover, and improved performance. They increased their annual sales and profits by more than 20 percent compounded during the period from 1973 to 1978.

Characteristics

An organization where managers use positive practices has the following characteristics: (1) The organization's values are expressed and provide operational guidance; (2) the focus is on organization results; (3) the norms are supportive of positive practices; (4) accountability is managed; (5) people are empowered; (6) there is a supportive environment; and (7) there is high self-worth among employees. Managers integrate and balance organizational needs and individual needs.

Organization Values. Value statements provide direction for the organization and individuals. With positive practices, they are expressed both verbally and in writing; they are operational; and they are supported by managers. When an organization clearly establishes and expresses certain beliefs and expects behavior and performance that support them, they provide a significant unifying force. We believe that the values-based management statement that Clarkson articulated for his organization's guidance helped to provide the impetus for turning Graphic Controls from a loss position to one of unprecedented growth and profit for the next seven years. His statement was:

> It seems clear to me that a business organization (or any other organization for that matter) can achieve superior results and produce greater work satisfaction and enjoyment for the people in it if there are more trust and openness, more sensitivity to the needs of the people, more opportunities to build self-confidence and feelings of importance, and more equality of rights and privileges in the organization structure. . . . A full-time person spends over 2,000 hours a year at this work place. It is important that [people] feel that their varied needs have a chance of being partially satisfied concurrent with the organization's needs being met. Thus, managers need to know what is truly rewarding for those who work for them. . . . An effective collaborative climate should provide members of the group with a high degree of participation in key decisions. This is easy, natural and understandable to experience, but very hard to develop. . . . The manager is responsible for building those that report to him into a group that makes high quality decisions and carries them out well [Alutto, 1978, p. 2].

Clarkson lived these values and constantly reminded his managers of them. This statement was operational at all times and was not just one of those speeches the boss makes on a special occasion and then files away to be forgotten. The latter happens in a negative environment emphasizing the attitude that "nothing will change," "it's useless," or "nobody cares." Values, both organizational and individual, are treated in depth in Chapter One.

Organization Results. Managers using positive practices have a strong focus on organization results. This means that achieving results for the organization is primary, and individual jobs or functions are secondary. For instance, the accounting function's result would be informed financial decisions, and the maintenance engineer's result would be equipment that is available for production, as compared with the activity of maintaining equipment. A more detailed explanation of this result orientation is presented in Chapter Two. When managers are held accountable for organization results, they become aware that they have to work with other people in order to be successful. The accountant has to work with line managers to be sure that financial reports are useful for making financial decisions. The maintenance engineer must work closely with the operators of the equipment to assure its availability when needed.

The results orientation also forces managers to be sure that the activities of their units are contributing to the achievement of the company's mission. With this focus, managers will think organization first and their function second. This will bring all functions to focus on common goals and cooperation to satisfy the needs of customers or clients. Results also form a basis for evaluating the performance of individuals and units. Commitment and motivation are fostered when people see that what they do serves others and is meaningful to the success of the enterprise. Chapter Three provides ways to clarify the role relationships that are necessary to accomplish organization results.

The focus on organization results makes it imperative that there be clarity of roles among those working for a common result. Where there is no accountability for organization results, the need for role clarification is not evident. For instance, if sales is accountable only for selling, production for producing, and customer service for serving, there is little or no coordination. Sales may sell a product that production cannot fully produce, and customer service may have continuous problems in making the product or service right for the customer. When sales, production, and customer service are held jointly accountable for customer satisfaction, they have to talk to each other and cooperate to assure that the customers are getting the product that will fulfill their needs. This makes it necessary that the people in these functions clarify their roles or working relationships: how they are going to work together, give feedback, communicate, negotiate, support, and manage accountability. This is a new experience for many managers, requiring new skills and approaches.

Role clarification has to take place between managers and subordinates and between team members. We find very few conflicts that are really personality conflicts—they are usually role conflicts. In consulting with organizations, one of the first steps is to clarify roles to reduce conflict. This process will eliminate overlap and duplication of duties as well as uncover gaps where responsibility for certain tasks has not been assigned or accepted. Chapter Three goes into detail on how a manager can achieve role clarification and maintain it. This process increases organizational effectiveness and provides the basis for managing support and accountability.

Commitment to organization results and role clarification will free energy to increase productivity. Managers can influence the quality—positive or negative—of this energy and how it is utilized. Positive energy is characterized by hopefulness, helpfulness, powerfulness, opportunities, choices, and change. The energy of individuals is focused on accomplishing organization goals and, when used with the energy of others, can have a synergistic effect. Positive energy creates high motivation. On the other hand, negative energy is a depleter, characterized by hopelessness, helplessness, powerlessness, no opportunities, no choices, and no change. There is resistance to accomplishing things for the organization. Managers can transform negative energy to positive by the way they manage and communicate with people. Transformation tools and techniques are described in Chapter Four. When there is positive energy present, people have confidence and the will to solve any problem facing them.

Norms. The culture of an organization has to be examined when managers decide to change their behavior. One of the key cultural influences on successful change is norms—both informal and formal rules about how things are done. They may be spoken or unspoken. For instance, a norm in one organization may be "never disagree with the boss" or "you don't confront the boss." People have learned that they get punished if they violate these norms. This may be generalized to the point where no one confronts anyone on broken agreements or unsatisfactory performance. If this norm exists, it will be a barrier to instituting positive practices. When managers decide to use positive practices, they will have to deliberately work at changing the norm of "not confronting" to one of "confrontation is practiced and expected." They will have to model this new behavior by confronting others themselves and accepting confrontation without defensiveness or retribution.

Other normative areas are training, orientation, allocation of rewards, allocation of resources, communications, and interactions and relationships. Each of these should be examined to determine whether they are supportive of establishing a positive environment. This can be determined by a survey of people at all levels in the organization. If they are not supportive, objectives should be set to change them. If this deliberate action is not taken, the organization will revert to its old ways of doing things. We have witnessed this in instituting management by objectives for results (MBO/R) and organization development (OD). After training sessions, managers leave with enthusiasm and good intentions to use the new concepts. Twelve months later, a visit to the organization will discover that there is little trace of use of the new concepts, because the old norms gradually blocked them. The influence of these cultural norms and how they can be changed are discussed in Chapter Five.

Accountability. Accountability is a cornerstone of positive practices. The willingness of a manager to hold people accountable for their behavior and to be held accountable him- or herself is essential for organizational effectiveness. Managing accountability is a key positive practice. People need to be clear on their roles and expectations of each other and have clear agreements that are the basis for holding each other accountable.

Support and accountability need to be managed together. For instance, a manager holds a subordinate accountable for satisfactory performance. In confronting an unsatisfactory performer, the manager must be open to the possibility that he or she did not give the employee the support needed for satisfactory performance or did not make his or her standards or expectations clear to the subordinate. Chapter Six suggests a system to help a manager handle such a situation.

The use of positive practices requires a manager to be both sensitive and tough-minded in the way he or she confronts subordinates and others when there is a problem or concern. Confrontation is often avoided or handled in a destructive manner in both organizational and personal life. It is an emotionally laden process, which may have many negative connotations as a result of earlier experiences in personal or work life. Under positive practices, confrontation is viewed as a positive experience with positive results. We suggest that a manager look at confrontation as a caring effort—caring for the other person, the relationship, and the success of the organization—and for the self as well, since the avoidance of confrontation can be stressful. Chapter Seven deals with confrontation and gives managers suggestions on how to handle the process in a caring, supportive, and tough-minded manner.

Empowerment. Managers using positive practices will empower both themselves and their employees to more fully utilize their skills and competencies. In a positive environment, people feel free to speak out with their ideas. Individuals empower each other through straight communications, confrontation, and a focus on the positive. Two of the essentials of empowerment are self-confidence and confidence and trust in others, which reduce the fear and insecurity that often exist in organizations. Fear and guilt block people from using their power freely to accomplish things for the organization. When individuals empower themselves, they empower others. This becomes exciting when positive energy is flowing freely. The results are high motivation and synergism. This subject, with suggestions on how to accomplish it, is covered in Chapter Eight.

When employees are empowered, their creative skills are available to the organization. All of us are creative, but most of us are not using these skills because of barriers that we have placed within ourselves or that we perceive in our environment. Often our perceptions are not accurate, but we do not test the situation to check their validity. In using positive practices, a manager will encourage and support creative ideas from anywhere in the organization. Concepts such as quality circles, when supported by management, have shown us that people at all levels in the organization are creative. When employees learn that their ideas on improving their jobs and their work environment are wanted and are implemented, they are free and eager to offer them. However, when they are put down for their suggestions or receive no response, they soon learn that their ideas are not wanted. Where managers reject or sit on suggestions, quality circles fail and become recreation and relaxation activities instead of a productive motivating force for the workers. Chapter Nine gives managers ways to identify barriers and stimulate creativity in themselves and the work force.

Support. As mentioned earlier, support has to be managed along with accountability. Managers using positive practices constantly look for ways to support their employees. They check regularly to see that they are getting the support they need from management and that team members and units in the organization are supporting each other. Cooperation and teamwork become a norm in the organization.

In a positive environment, managers see their relationships with others as interdependent. In other words, people are using their power with others. In some more traditional organizations, people are dependent on others for power or use their power either against others or independently, without regard for others. To accomplish teamwork, managers must be aware of their own as well as team members' needs for interpersonal skills. They must let team members know how they wish them to operate with each other in support and accountability. They may use an outside consultant on team building if they find that they are unable to accomplish this themselves. Support and how to establish it are discussed in Chapter Ten.

Self-Worth. This last characteristic of positive practices is the most important. It is the undergirding of all the other characteristics. High self-worth starts with managers who feel good about and take good care of themselves. Such managers act to build self-worth in their subordinates and others around them. In transactional-analysis terms, they keep themselves in the "I am OK with me/you are OK with me" life position. When they fall into a "not OK" position, they do not remain there long, as it is dysfunctional in problem solving and in dealing with others in the straight and honest way that establishes trust. The first step in developing high self-worth is to get clear with yourself about who you are as a human being while being aware of your wants. This is dealt with in Chapter Eleven, which presents ways to manage yourself in a positive manner.

Managers with high self-worth are more inclined to take care of themselves physically, psychologically, and spiritually and manage the stress in their lives more effectively. This positive practice is essential for staying healthy and using energy in a positive manner. Stress is a twentieth-century disease that, if not managed effectively, can cause physical and mental harm. This, of course, has considerable effect on productivity for the organization. A manager needs to be aware of the stress in his or her life, both at home and at work, and develop his or her own holistic program for managing it constructively. Such a program values working with the physical, psychological, and spiritual parts of one's being. Chapter Twelve will help a manager to become aware of the potentially harmful effects of stress and to develop a program for keeping healthy.

Chapter Thirteen provides further help in managing stress and developing practices that will program managers for positive energy. Meditation, affirmations, and visualization and imagery are practices that can be used to enhance positive thinking and attitudes. They are tools and techniques that help individuals change negative thoughts and attitudes. They are also ways to change any negative programming that may have developed. For instance, some people came to believe early in life that they were not creative as a result of how they were treated at home, school, or church. They may have had negative experiences in art or writing that led them to this decision. Once they are aware of this, they can use the techniques described in Chapter Thirteen to reprogram themselves so that their creative skills are available to them.

Implementation

Any manager can start using positive practices wherever he or she is in the organization. Of course, it is much easier when there is a supportive environment for the new behavior. Consequently, a manager who uses some of these positive practices must at the same time work deliberately to build a supportive environment that will accept the new behavior and reward it. Support groups and objectives to change norms that are barriers are two tools to use.

Naturally, it is easier if positive practices are used by top management. If this is not the case, the next best place is the manager of a semiautonomous unit, such as a plant, a district, or a region. Other managers will have to determine for themselves which practices they can put into effect without the support of upper management. An honest evaluation will reveal that many of these positive practices can be used without much formality. The use of a support group is probably essential. It is difficult to change behavior without the support of at least one person who will compliment you when you behave as you wish to and confront you when you do not. In any event, it will require patience, persistence, and perseverance to achieve permanent behavior change.

After determining what you wish to change, the next step is to identify the barriers to that change—not only in the environment but also within yourself—and then develop the strategies to eliminate or reduce them. It is also recommended that you not change too much too fast. Take one new practice, get it under your belt with comfort, then take on another. As you progress, you will find the task getting easier with each new practice. There probably will be a need for some supportive training, either within the organization or externally, through seminars and workshops. Building self-worth is essential for handling fear, insecurity, and guilt, the big stoppers. The use of external consulting services is often a must for getting started.

If a manager wishes to establish these positive practices in his or her organization, steps similar to these should be followed. Training for all managers is essential. It is preferable that the training be carried out with two and three levels of management involved in the same session. This allows for new working agreements to be established. To maintain the new behavior, other normative areas that must be established are rewards, orientation, communications, allocation of resources, and modeled behavior. Detailed suggestions on implementation are summarized in the Conclusion.

It is our desire and hope that you, the manager, will move through this book assessing where you are in your own management practices, being aware of what is working for you and what is not. Using this information, you can select some of the suggested practices and develop your own plan for implementation, one or two practices at a time. Implementation will be easier if you use a support group to work with you. It will be more productive if you use this book with your team and the group makes decisions on which practices you wish to implement. Whatever change you decide to make, we recommend that you set objectives with a plan of action and checkpoints to evaluate your progress. This book warrants more than just one reading. It will serve as a ready reference for options when you have a problem that is not being solved by your usual approach. In any event, we want you to enjoy managing as a positive and satisfying experience.

⚘ 1 ⚘

Values
Set the Stage
for Performance

⚘ ⚘ ⚘ ⚘ ⚘ ⚘ ⚘ ⚘

Forward-looking managers in today's fast-action organizations and changing environment have to make frequent choices about their direction. A variety of both functional and managerial issues may be involved. To create and maintain a positive organizational situation in such an operating environment, managers need to be aware of the beliefs, or values, that are guiding their decisions. An American Management Association report (Schmidt and Posner, 1982) described values as a powerful (though often silent) force in organizational life, since values will most likely determine which facts are examined with care and which are passed over lightly, which options for action are looked upon with favor from the start and which are rejected out of hand. Values are significant for you as a manager because they provide the basis for what you perceive to be right or wrong, good or bad, and what you are for or against. Values are particularly significant in relationships and, thus, in the functioning of communications in the organization. By understanding more about the values that are operational in the organization and among individuals, you are able to improve your communications and managerial effectiveness.

Several books that have been widely read by managers pointed out some other significant applications for values. *In Search of Excellence* (Peters and Waterman, 1982), *Megatrends* (Naisbitt, 1982), and *Corporate Cultures* (Deal and Kennedy, 1982) each provided new awareness of the organizational impact of values in the decision-making and implementation processes. Particularly at the executive management level, value choices have a major impact on direction. As pointed out in these books, clarity of direction is a positive factor in organizations. The currently growing literature on organization culture emphasizes the need for managers throughout the organization to develop clear statements about the values that are important to the performance of the organization and its subunits. As the manager of any of these organizational groupings, you are responsible for providing a useful clarification process and clearly articulating a set of values that provide managerial guidance for operations. In this chapter are some examples of what those statements might be like, further discussions of their importance and contribution to the organization, and some techniques to work with in setting the stage for more focused organizational performance.

Foundation for Performance

Management and organization literature does not include much about organization values. During research for this chapter, our computer search found, for instance, in excess of 19,000 references for "organization" and 14,000 for "values" but only 43 for "organization values." Most often, values are examined from the perspective of the individual only. As a manager places emphasis on achieving organization results as a positive practice, it also becomes necessary for him or her to consider values from the organization's perspective.

Values are like a cornerstone, or a core, from which further growth emanates. At the organizational level, managers need to have a valuing process that will provide operational guidance for individuals throughout the organization. This requires acceptance of the organization as a "body" that has a unique set of values or an underlying philosophy that the individual is willing to share or assume as a member. Such a shared commitment is frequently the motivational basis for people working together to achieve inspired performance.

McCoy (1983, p. 24) points out that "an ethical corporate value system attempts to clarify what individuals are supposed to do and to reward them for doing it well. An understanding of the implicit values of an organization appears indispensable for individuals at all levels—from the employee for the fit of his or her values and those of the employer, to the president, whose role, implicitly or explicitly, encompasses the understanding and management of the corporate value system." He points out further that "To be consistent, a feedback system must integrate and legitimize the goals and objectives of the corporation and be self-correcting when there are changes to be made. When this system becomes unhinged or out of balance, confusion and stress result, primarily on the part of middle managers, who receive conflicting signals as to what is proper behavior."

Earlier publications included these thoughts about values themselves: "Values are normative views held by individual human beings (consciously or subconsciously) of what is good and desirable. They provide standards by which people are influenced in their choice of actions. Social values reflect a system of shared beliefs which serve as norms of human conduct" (Kast and Rosenzweig, 1974, pp. 154-155). "Values are the basis for deciding what one is for or against or where one is going and why. Values give direction to our lives and help establish our character. They have to do with our 'basic' or 'core' ways of behaving as we are in relationship with others and our environment. From only a few dozen basic values our attitudes and beliefs flow out and are experienced as actions relative to some subject, issue, or situation" (Beck and Hillmar, 1976, p. 7).

Values are not absolutes. They are subjective, preferred states that guide action choices and become observable or identifiable through behavior that reflects how we see our world fitting together. These beliefs—or values—are our notions about the existence of a relationship between two things; for example, the quality of life depends on developing a value system that emphasizes cooperation and the improvement of the total human community. If this quality-of-life premise is accepted as a guiding belief in the organization, the manager now has a guide to appropriate action choices, which should include cooperation and commitment to an improved human community.

Another illustration: If "purposeful" is an organization value, managers validate their condition or preferred state of being "purposeful" by the existence of planned activity directed toward producing specific outcomes. Implementation of this organization value could be further verified by asking, "How is that planned activity being managed throughout the organization?" It is in consistently and supportively translating these broader generalizations into detailed actions that most organizations—and managers—have difficulty. When an organization, working group, or team develops and states a set of values that establishes *preferred* modes of conduct, they have a value-system statement that becomes the basis for managerial guidance and accountability.

Organization values are those shared beliefs or values that, as a set, describe the operational philosophy and provide the basis for the organization's purpose. Key to the operational reality of organization values is the continual monitoring of the consistency among assumptions, philosophy, purpose, and practice. It is this feedback loop that regularly asks and validates: Are we (as a group) living out our beliefs? As measured by what? Does our way of working together include a regular sharing of values among organizational levels? Is there a reasonable fit between organizational values and individual values? Are our goals consistent with our values?

Clarkson (1982), in presenting a case study of his management process at Graphic Controls Corporation, described how his corporate management group used five value-system concepts to develop a list of behavioral characteristics that they then set out to implement fully. The concepts were: the authority of knowledge rather than power; the sharing of power and decision-making authority while retaining individual accountability; the commitment resulting from effective involvement and participation; the need for individual *and* group responsibility; and informed choice. From their discussions of those concepts, they developed the following list of desired characteristics for organizational behavior: trusting, confidential, spontaneous, constructive, nonpunitive, confronting, intellectually honest, nonjudgmental, nondefensive, risk-taking, emotionally honest, caring, creative, innovative, playful, committed, adaptable, candor, and openness. During the ten-year implementation period described in the case, annual sales and income increased approximately 20 percent compounded, while the number of employees almost tripled. Implementing these characteristics also led to significant changes in the quality of work life and recognition through the Phillips Award for Outstanding Management-Labor Relations in 1979.

Another example of how organizational statements of values are being used by managers is presented by Kiefer and Senge (1984). Analog Devices, Inc. (ADI) is described as a manufacturer of analogue-digital converters and related devices for computerized measurement and control systems. The company has grown at a rate of 30 percent a year for the past five years (1983 sales of about $220 million), thanks in large part to a clear corporate philosophy that values the contribution of each individual. ADI's value statement could have been taken from any of the organizations we have studied: "(1) We believe people are honest and trustworthy, and that they want to be treated with dignity and respect. (2) They want to achieve their full potential, and they'll work hard to do so. (3) They want to understand the purpose of their work and the goals of the organization they serve. (4) They want a strong hand in determining what to do and how to do it. (5) They want to be accountable for results and to be recognized and rewarded for their achievements" (Kiefer and Senge, 1984, p. 74). Relatively few cases concerning the impact of organization values have been formally researched and documented. However, as with the cases described here, the positive anecdotal evidence that correlates with increased organizational performance is growing.

Significance in Today's Environment

Increasing attention has been given in recent years to the significance of values in organizational life. The evidence is supportive of our belief that more conscious values applications lead to significant organizational and managerial contributions. The most widely distributed support comes through *In Search of Excellence* (Peters and Waterman, 1982, p. 280), which states that "every excellent company we studied is clear on what it stands for, and takes the process of value shaping seriously . . . it appeared that not only the articulation of values but also the content of those values (and probably the way they are said) makes the difference."

Through values-based organizational statements, managers can create the foundation and guidance for positive practices. Such statements set the tone for the behaviors and organizational performance expected. Management's value positions must be carried down through the whole organization. When higher levels of management do not set value standards for the organization, it is important that each manager does so for his or her own work group's guidance.

Value choices also make a significant contribution to the organization's vision and goal statements, as described in Chapter Two; its role-clarification activity, as discussed in Chapter Three; and its standards of accountability, as presented in Chapter Six. Since our values influence almost every aspect of our work experience, there is a wide variety of application areas that are important for both internal and external operations. Some examples follow.

Decision Making. This is the primary application. Our values directly influence the decisions we make in our work activities. For example, we are more likely to make conservative decisions when *security* is valued than when *growth* or *risk taking* is valued. When we have no clear organizational guidance, some level of indecision is likely to slow down the decision process until someone chooses to act independently, which may cause additional problems.

Direction. Another basic attribute of values is that they

provide focused direction. If *caring, supportive,* or *structured* behavior is one of your organization values, you will have to examine your tasks and relationships to verify that you and others are behaving in what is considered to be an appropriate way.

Cohesiveness. Clustered around cohesiveness and overlapping with other areas are several related items. Values facilitate the choice of specific goals within an overall scenario that describes the desired performance. When people have that direction available, the underlying values provide cohesiveness—a focusing and joining together—because of their importance to the individuals. This is especially true when they are also perceived as providing hope for the future and are worthy of praise. The potential for such action is much higher when those involved are committed to behaviors associated with the value *supportive.*

Management Style. McGregor (1960, p. 33) used the phrase "assumptions about human nature and human behavior" to describe the value sets that are the driving forces for two different approaches to managing people and organizations: directive (Theory X) and participative (Theory Y). Since each person's experience has given him or her a different perspective on specific behaviors associated with each of the management styles, it is important that each manager come to an understanding of those things that are personally important in order to be able to work within those beliefs. It is through discussing these concerns that managers get shared understanding, trust, and commitment. In a similar way, we could go on through such areas as motivation, organization structure, policy making, strategic choices in marketing and operations, and growth and change to analyze underlying value sets and develop behaviors that will be in accord with the expressed values.

Having worked with values at both the personal and organizational levels, we have experienced an increasing demand for clear value statements at the organizational level. Frequently, though, the concern is not presented as a value issue. People are interested in participating in their organization's process. Consequently, they want to know more than ever about the "why" and "how" of things. From working with this process for many years, we know that conscious and responsible development and implementation of the valuing process produce more positive results for both the organization and the individual.

Developing Clarity of Values

It is important to point out that managers should not seek to force a change in individuals' values when personal choice is appropriate. However, through fostering greater awareness of the organization's values and their relative importance and application patterns, we can negotiate supportive behavior patterns that will not ordinarily compromise anyone's personal values. At the least, this process leads to a clearer understanding of human differences.

Getting Clear About Your Own Values. Organization values are usually based on those of the top manager or those shared by a top management group. Whether they originate in a directive or a participative manner, we believe that it is helpful for each manager (and person) to be aware of the values that are guiding his or her own behavior. There is no clear-cut, best way to do that; it is largely a matter of exploration. Since many management groups have done relatively little values clarification, we usually encourage managers to work on clarification in their natural work groups. We will identify several possibilities that can be used over time with a group. Using several approaches provides different perspectives. With any of these techniques, we believe that it is important to use the information as a basis for discussion and further exploration rather than to establish prescriptive absolutes. The primary issue is what you do with your preferences and how that affects your relationships. This human interaction makes it important that you share and discuss your position with members of your group. It is in this process of discussing your beliefs and what you do because of them that a rich potential comes to fruition. There we build trust levels, openness, acceptance of individuals, organizational spirit, and close personal relationships.

For a manager getting started with values clarification, there are some approaches that can be used without the assistance of an outside consultant or facilitator. In getting your work group to examine and explore what's important for them, you could use the following procedure.

Start with a listing of "value" words. This can be as simple as making a list of ten to fifteen words that describe the really important things for you in your organizational life, such as freedom, happiness, money, trust, integrity, cooperation, effectiveness, success, innovation, risk taking, responsibility, honesty, competence, excitement, and security. Once the words are down, define them or establish a rough statement of the meaning for each individual, since people vary in their understanding and usage of certain well-known terms. Typically, the next step is for each person to rank order his or her list of value words and then explain why that order was chosen. Finally, the group can move to talking about the items, their definition, their order, and their meaning in your way of thinking.

The manager usually leads the discussion and exploration of values. If the group is large, you can break into smaller groups for initial work and then come back together for summary presentation and discussion. The important thing here is to get as full a discussion and understanding as possible for each individual. When there is some question about a point, clarification should be sought without any suggestion of belittling the person. Discuss the responses to "How come those choices in that order top and bottom?", and explore with each other your own ideas on how this information can be used to make your relationship and understanding of each other more supportive and productive for your organization. As individuals clarify more of their own information with others in the group, the distinction between individual and group begins to blur. Once an individual has clarified his or her data, that information is available for sharing by the group. Ultimately, the manager will bring the appropriate beliefs together in a form that will provide a clear statement for the group's guidance and direction.

Exhibit 1, developed by organization consultant Richard S. Underhill, provides a structured option to be used in much the same way as the practice just presented. Values can be added or deleted as appropriate. Remember that, in addition to

Exhibit 1. Ranking Form for Organizational Values.

What I value in organizations that I belong to is for the organization to be (please number, from highest of 1 to lowest of 19, in order of importance to you):

_____ A. *Achieving*—making a worthwhile contribution to the larger society and meeting the needs of individuals.

_____ B. *Balanced*—maintaining appropriate concern for the needs of society, the organization, and individuals without discounting any of the three.

_____ C. *Beautiful*—having a sense of the esthetic in its architecture, landscaping, and work environment.

_____ D. *Caring*—making people important and being concerned with their health and well-being.

_____ E. *Comfortable*—providing a place where people fit easily, relate to one another well, and feel that they are wanted.

_____ F. *Egalitarian*—providing equal opportunity for all and access to the information needed to control their own lives.

_____ G. *Exciting*—offering stimulating, active opportunities for individuals to risk, to grow, to express themselves.

_____ H. *Free*—providing a place where members can make choices, express their independence, and participate in decisions that affect their lives and careers.

_____ I. *Fulfilling*—having a sense that the work is meaningful and the organization contributes to society as the individual contributes to the organization—a place where I want to go to work.

_____ J. *Harmonious*—fostering inter- and intragroup harmony, given to solving problems rather than blaming and finding fault.

_____ K. *Humanistic*—being concerned more with contributing to human welfare and the quality of life than the competitive struggle for markets and a standard of living.

_____ L. *Integrated*—possessing unity and wholeness beyond a simple summing of the parts—the parts have a working relationship.

_____ M. *Purposeful*—having a clear sense of organization purpose—a mission—that we are committed to and use to evaluate all our results and activities.

_____ N. *Spontaneous*—being responsive to needs, flexible, open to change, not bound by strong traditions when they are not functional.

_____ O. *Structured*—living by a clear set of policies, rules, and procedures that state what is expected of individuals and how they should behave.

_____ P. *Supportive*—supplying the necessary resources, tools, equipment, and training to get the job done; my boss gets me what I need and encourages me.

_____ Q. *Secure*—being strong enough that I am not worrying about being laid off or fired for no fault of my own.

Exhibit 1. Ranking Form for Organizational Values, Cont'd.

____ R. *Successful*—being a leader in its field with a good growth and profit (service) record; well established.

____ S. *Warm*—encouraging friendly and informal relations, emphasis on enjoying fellowship.

Source: Adapted from the form "Values I Seek in My Organization," by Richard S. Underhill. Used by permission.

focusing on the desired goal direction, the values discussion and interaction are expected to provide substantial direction for defining appropriate behavior for achieving high performance.

The "Values for Working" questionnaire (Flowers, Hughes, Myers, and Myers, 1975) provides another way of thinking about values that we have found to be useful in working with managers and their groups. In this way of looking at things, people have value positions about issues such as type of supervision, job freedom, money, type of work, and rules and regulations that cause them to behave with predictable patterns. The different values that people hold on the type of boss they like are presented by Hughes and Flowers (1978) and adapted slightly here. Which of the statements listed below would describe best your own preference(s)? If you were to spread twelve points among the possibilities, how would it come out?

1. One who tells employees exactly what to do, how to do it, and encourages employees by doing it with them.
2. One who is tough, but allows employees to be tough, too.
3. One who calls the shots and is not always changing his or her mind, and sees to it that everyone follows the rules.
4. One who does not ask questions as long as employees get the job done.
5. One who gets employees working together in close harmony by being more of a friendly person than a boss.
6. One who gives employees access to the information needed and lets them do the job in their own way.

Source: Hughes and Flowers, 1978. © 1978 by Center for Values Research, Inc., 8848 Greenville Ave., Dallas, Texas, 75243-1082 (214-553-8848). Used by permission.

Now, examine your response for what it says about your preference in management style. If, as a manager, you were strongly
oriented toward the statements in items 4 or 5, how do you
manage a subordinate whose expectations are strongly oriented
toward item 3? This is not an unusual situation in many of today's organizations, and it highlights the need for positive practices in accepting and working with the differences in individuals. We believe that it is most appropriate to manage the other
person primarily on the basis of what they need or want, not
what you believe. Clarifying such differences of expectation is a
fundamental concern in the process of developing an operational value system. Having described how you believe things
should be on the issues presented in the questionnaire and having shared them with your work group as described in the previous practices, you, the manager, are able to establish a much
clearer set of work expectations, built on that understanding
and your concern for individual needs and values.

Sharing for Openness and Trust. It has been our experience while working with teams and work groups that they develop greater openness and trust through values-clarification
efforts if they continue to work with them over time. This effort should not be just a one-time happening that is quickly
forgotten. It is important to acknowledge how people's values
differ and to work with those differences. Whatever our beliefs, they affect our relationships and the organization's positive performance. When we, as a working group, openly discuss
things that are important to us in the context of our situation,
we are building more support and trust. For each of us in organizations, the true test is how open and trusting our own
behavior with others is. How a working team can use values
clarification to facilitate openness and trust is illustrated by the
following experience.

A young, newly appointed manager was experiencing considerable resistance from his management team of nine older, long-term subordinates
and staff members from a subdivision of a larger
national organization. As part of a two-day team-

building and "clear the air" retreat, we began with organization values clarification. Using the organization values list presented as Exhibit 1, each person ranked the list to reflect his or her own preferences. In three clusters, they shared their ranking and discussed why that particular arrangement was important for them. Then they worked for agreement on what the top five organization values were, as voiced in their group, and developed a tentative ranking or order of importance from their discussions. The three listings were:

Group A	Group B	Group C
Fulfilling	Spontaneous	Purposeful
Harmonious	Secure	Warm
Caring	Comfortable	Balanced
Purposeful	Supportive	Harmonious
Supportive	Humanistic	Fulfilling

Each cluster was then asked to create a scenario or verbal picture of how they would like their organization to function to live out the value system that they had just defined. Further, they were asked to describe as specifically as possible who would be doing what—that is, to describe specific behaviors that would be expected of individuals to make their scenario operational on a day-to-day basis. The groups found it relatively easy to rank the value words but considerably more difficult to convert those idealized generalizations into specific, observable ways to live out values preferences.

The groups were coming together productively as they shared their ideas about how things would be done, though the process was not without some rough edges. The behavior of a member who continued to work with her needlepoint throughout the session was not perceived as appropriate for a good relationship with her peers. However, that conflict of expectations was not resolved during this "opening" session, which was kept mostly at the level of organizational issues, which is usual for beginning explorations within a working group.

Most individuals were willing to express their feelings about the organization and desires for the future. Through these increasingly open expressions, people were developing and experiencing more trust and support. They took more risk to identify problem areas and individuals. They also found that they were not alone—as some had feared—in their perception of some things that were not helpful for the organization's performance. By the time they were involved in the task of scenario building, they were more comfortable with sharing deeper-level concerns and desires.

When the clusters came back together after several hours of intensive work, they were excited about hearing each other's presentations in order to really get the organization focused. They expressed a strong and sincere desire to get things together and get on with achieving satisfactory performance. In sharing what they had developed with each other, they showed a significant level of ownership of and identity) with the evolving organizational picture. There was intense listening and seeking for understanding, which minimized the urge to be defensive on some points. Time was taken to do some problem solving on specific issues needing attention. Other items were scheduled for continuing work "back home." Through the sharing process, the group members developed an increased willingness to be open about issues and their feelings about them and to be supportive of each other in their resolution. The whole team was drawn together in a cohesive and energizing way through its focusing on items identified as representing what the organization was "all about" and identifying areas where they needed to put their energy in their future movement toward excellence.

The group left with much greater clarity about a number of issues concerning the performance of various units. It also went forward with a rekindled "spirit" from having shared in developing a belief system for guiding their activities. They strongly affirmed that the outcome was well worth the time and effort spent in achieving it. This same openness, spirit, and trust were maintained within the group and continued to mature after they were back to their usual work. Several months later, participants considered this values-clarification effort a significant event in the life of this work team.

Positive practices such as the values-clarification efforts described here are the essence of participative teamwork. They produce highly focused group energy and commitment that lead to clarity of direction and goals for action. It is in this type of organizational work that the foundation is established for positive management and excellence. As the manager, you have your team engaged in setting expectations for organizational and individual performance. Everyone will know what it takes to "make it" here and why that is important.

Having a set of values establishes positions on issues that are critical to the development of an organization's strategic and operational goals. With such choices in hand, a manager is in a more informed position for entering the planning process. The following chapter describes positive practices that lead to a statement of an organizational vision supported by tightly focused goals. These will provide organizational guidance and direction based on values, the things that are important for the work group or organization.

2

Providing Direction with Positive Vision and Goals

One of the most demanding challenges facing today's managers —particularly top managers—is focusing the energies within the organization in such a way that groups and individuals have a clear path to inspired performance. In this chapter, we will examine some positive actions that managers can take to provide that type of direction. The practices discussed here are important for the whole organization, not just individuals. Establishing the organization's vision, purpose, and goal statements is a fundamental effort in its planning process. These statements, which define the organization's reason for being and provide basic operating direction, are based on clarified value and philosophical choices as described in Chapter One. These are positive practices in the managerial process and must be managed at each level in the organization. As manager, it is your responsibility to make sure that your organization and subordinates have the necessary direction to enable a high level of performance. It is here that "dreams" get translated into the specific action commitments leading to the organization's desired accomplishment.

Though all of these planning functions can be done with a group process, we find that the top or senior manager in each organization or subunit usually establishes the outline of the vision for that group. Then, others are involved in building and refining the details of its implementation. This personal involvement generally creates a higher level of individual commitment to achieving the desired results.

Organization Results

A significant change that we have found necessary here is a shift in thinking from a focus on individual results to one on organization results as the primary reference point. We have found that the term *results* is typically used to refer to individual achievement, though frequently in an organizational context: "What counts here are results!" As we stated in *Making MBO/R Work* (Beck and Hillmar, 1976), we believe that managers and employees at all levels must look first to the organization's accomplishment, for that is where accountability for results must be established. It is the organization's accomplishment or outcome condition that managers need to focus on for developing the individual's commitment to specific contributions. IBM's often referred to goal—the best customer service of any company in the world—provides a very clear point of reference for direction within the organization. A comparable top-management statement for your organization can be expected to have a similar cohesive force, though, certainly, each situation has its own set of conditions that affect the result statement.

Managers with the traditional orientation often referred to as a closed-system perspective tend to direct things from their own knowledge, looking downward and inward to make sure that everything is functioning right internally. In thinking and working from an organization-results point of view, managers must become more conscious of how the functioning of the organization is being affected by forces coming from higher levels in the organization or from outside. Then they will look upward and outward to determine how to work with clients, customers, or resources in order to achieve the desired outcome. We think that such a change in perspective is essential for the shift from an efficiency to an effectiveness orientation and that its limited implementation is one of the major reasons that efficiency continues to be the dominant consideration.

When a manager focuses on efficiency, the concern is centered on internal activities and rates of production, since the ratio of production to input is the primary indicator of efficiency. Here is the key to rewards in most organizations, where the working assumption is that "management" should be happy as long as efficiency is maintained. However, when the focus is on effectiveness, the manager's main concern is what the subgroup should be doing to satisfy a customer's or user's need or desire. In this case, the manager looks outward or upward to determine whether the organization is meeting this need, as customer satisfaction is an indicator of effectiveness. It is still important that the group be concerned with efficiency, but only after identifying the desired final results. A manager needs to maintain a high level of awareness of the effectiveness of his or her group's performance and how that is contributing to the realization of the organization's goals. Until those goals are clearly defined and tied back to day-to-day actions, there will be little basis for holding a manager accountable primarily for effectiveness, rather than efficiency.

The impact of such changes in thinking is often very subtle but can be very dramatic. A recent demonstration illustrated what a difference the result orientation can make. An individual was asked to stiffen her arm and seek to stop the instructor from bending it at the elbow. When he grasped her arm, with one hand just above the elbow and one hand at the wrist, and exerted pressure, he was able to bend the arm at the elbow without much force. Then she was instructed to think of her arm as a long steel bar that could not be bent. When she had that "vision" in mind, the instructor tried again to bend the arm at the elbow in the same manner as before. This time, however, he was unable to do it, even with significantly more effort.

To many, such a shift in focus seems to be of little importance. We think it is of major importance, for it can affect the outcome as dramatically as just described. In the first try, the focus was on the activity of providing resistance and being efficient at that. For the second try, the focus was on the accomplishment. The same activity was a necessary part of the work, but it was now more clearly perceived as contributing to an accomplishment beyond itself. The effective use of all resources led to a different level of performance. Similarly, some organizations and groups we have worked with experienced significant differences when they changed their focus to producing organization results. Examples include a tax collection group that switched its focus from "receiving checks" (and holding them) to "funds available for use," an insurance organization that focused on "assured protection and security," and an educational system that focused on "problem-solving citizens."

Another aspect of changing management's way of thinking about organization results has to do with the manager's perception of performance and accomplishment. As mentioned above, when this is considered from an organizational point of view, the outcome occurs beyond a manager's operating area and has to be considered in terms of the satisfaction of customer, client, or user needs. This was a basic approach described by Drucker (1954) as part of his goal-setting process, which came to be known as management by objectives. It was presented in a slightly different way by Gilbert (1978, p. 17), who describes worthy performance as performance "in which the value of the accomplishment exceeds the cost of the behavior." Organization results, our primary concern here, are the accomplishments or outcomes—consequences of the task behaviors—created by the contribution of the individuals and groups involved. For most managers, it is a significant shift to look to those accomplishments as the basis for their performance accountability when they have usually been held accountable for carrying out tasks efficiently.

But how are you to establish the basis for evaluating the accomplishment? In Chapter One, we described how values are instrumental in defining and creating the scenario for the future. Being able to describe, clearly and specifically, the desired accomplishments that contribute to the realization of both or-

ganizational and individual achievements is the key to accountability for performance in attaining organization results. Such
clarity makes it possible to set the direction—goals, action plans,
performance standards, and similar planning guidance—that supports the establishment of responsibility for making something
happen. When you are able to clearly express expectations and
describe the relationships necessary for their achievement, all
parties can identify and coordinate the efforts necessary for accomplishment. To the extent that those accomplishments or
consequences are also experienced as laudable, hopeful, or to
the good of those involved, we will have a positive environment.
In the following sections, we will describe ways to work with
these issues.

Application Techniques

Alternative Futures. It is our belief that managers at all
levels, especially top managers, need to develop and choose
among alternative futures. When a positive, participative management style is used, such activity is likely to be general practice with managers. Sharing in the definition of the desired
future accomplishment, participating in the choice of that alternative, and creatively developing the plan for implementation
are managerial practices that build increased personal commitment and excitement about work. The management group of a
small manufacturing organization that has been implementing
the practices described in this book recently held a two-day development planning retreat. They included people from all functional areas, instead of just the general manager and top managers from marketing and production, as in the past. The whole
group was unusually excited about the quality and depth of the
plan that was produced as well as the continuing action commitments. When asked what was different about this experience that made it better than earlier practice, most identified
their personal involvement in the process of defining the organization's future as well as their own.

The approach that we use in developing alternative futures was developed by organization consultant R. S. Underhill,
who has contributed to our own growth in working with a fu-

ture orientation. Creating a vision of the future that provides a reference point for setting organization and individual goals is fundamental work for a manager at any level in the organization. Yet we have experienced a lack of clarity about future organization results with managers at all levels in organizations. In Chapter One, we discussed establishing organization values that can be used to clarify choices and make decisions necessary for creating a vision that includes the things considered important to operations. Values chosen might include trust, achievement, creativity, respect for human dignity, and cooperation. A manager exploring alternative futures for a group that has listed these values might discuss such questions as:

- How would you rank the order of importance of these five values?
- These values fall into the categories of productive performance (creativity and achievement) and human or personal behaviors. Which of those two is more important? (The choice here begins to define whether the emphasis is on production or on people, which might affect implementation and application issues later.)
- In considering application of the values preferences to a characteristic such as interpersonal relationships, how would you and the group expect the values to be translated into action?

By way of example, your group might respond with some initial statements such as these:

- We will focus on being creatively productive while building trust and cooperation into our relationships, in which the respect for human dignity or personhood is a significant concern.
- We will relate with others in ways that bring creative achievement to all of our productive efforts.
- We will do things together with openness to build trust and work together with cooperation by keeping each other informed and freely sharing information and ideas.
- Respect for the individual's human dignity will be shown

through acceptance of individuals involved with us in varied projects, using their ideas along with our own, and providing frequent recognition for items of merit.

When the group has expressed their choices or expectations, they could be asked to describe, as clearly and specifically as possible, who they would expect to be doing what tasks.

Having discussed such topics in some depth to explore the likes and dislikes, expectations, and wants of the members, you and the working group will have developed agreements about the basic structure of the preferred alternative future. This may remain as informal understandings, or it may be stated as a written agreement. In a variety of formats, such statements have come to be known as a superordinate goal, the vision, the future scenario, and, more traditionally, the mission or purpose statement.

Visioning

An American Management Association study has indicated that an ability to make diagnostic use of concepts is an important ingredient in managerial competence (Hayes, 1980). To have sufficient conceptual ability to take today's information and describe how it is likely to flow within the structure of the organization's operations—even as they might evolve—is a very powerful and desirable skill for managers. Enhancing one's abilities in this area requires a theory base, or road map, for understanding the meaning of the many things that are happening through individual and organizational behavior. This provides a reasonable basis for predicting what is likely to happen if you do certain things. Developing alternative futures, as discussed in the previous section, provides an opportunity for these skills to be applied to advantage.

As manager, it is your responsibility to keep your work group, at any level in the hierarchy, focused toward a *purpose.* This has typically been done with a mission or purpose statement for the whole organization, occasionally with further subgroup statements down through the organization. Unfortunately, there has never been a consensus among business executives as to what a mission statement really should be or do. Some think of it as narrowly following the military model, while others think of it as broad and general. Some use it for a public relations approach, some for defining marketing objectives, and some for internal operational guidance. Frequently, mission is associated only with strategic planning and passed over rather quickly in order to get to the operational aspects of goal setting. The article "Corporate Soul-Searching" (Brown, 1984, p. 44) states: "A mission statement is a charter that defines the basic business or businesses in which the enterprise will engage, the types of products it will make or the services it will provide, the markets it will serve, and perhaps how the company will conduct its affairs." These examples were cited: "moving people and material vertically and horizontally over relatively short distances" (Otis Elevator Company); "to concentrate on the basic business of consumer paints, chemical coatings, and specialty coatings, to continue as one of the 10 largest coatings companies in the country by growing internally and by acquisition" (the Valspar Corporation).

Schein (1985, p. 52) describes the development of a *mission* statement as resolving the problem of "obtaining a shared understanding of core mission, primary task, manifest and latent functions." He goes on to point out that a useful way to think about the ultimate or core mission is to ask, "What is our function in the larger scheme of things?" This perspective on mission and the increased concern for strategic aspects of the mission statement have led to more comprehensive statements, which we identify as scenarios, or vision statements. They are intended primarily to provide guidance in the internal managerial process and to focus the energy of the organization on clearly defined accomplishments and ways of doing things, such as might have been identified in what we have described as alternative futures.

Odiorne (1978, p. 1) defined a *scenario* as "a verbal picture describing the future in stylistic and verbal imagery . . . not just a verbal pipe dream, but a statement of conditions that would exist if the organization arrives at some future state successfully." Such a statement provides a distinctive path to follow into the future. These are not goal or objectives statements; rather, they have to be supported by specific, measurable performance objectives and action plans that assure the realization of the outcome described. An approach to developing a scenario would include the following steps: Describe the situation as you look from now to the future; list various alternative futures and describe the most likely effects with each situation; identify the limits and constraints within which you expect to operate as you move into the future that you want; choose the alternative future you want and integrate it with the situation and the limits expected. Odiorne went on to illustrate such alternatives and choices as these for the establishment of a new restaurant: "a place with character, not just a glass and steel burger place"; "a restored brick building in an older section of town, not a shopping center location"; "an 'Olde Towne' theme, style, and value orientation, including personnel in 1890s-type clothing, rather than a modern decor and theme."

An organization we have worked with developed this scenario: "Field work will be carried out by well-trained, well-paid, experienced employees who know exactly what the organization and local objectives are and who are given great latitude to use their best abilities to develop and accomplish these objectives. Personnel turnover will be held to a minimum, as salaries will equal those paid by other industries and the federal government. Attention will be given to the following motivators that provide job satisfaction: freedom, trust, support from above, self-esteem, achievement, personal growth, and recognition. We will increase our force by hiring more technicians from the local labor pool and will enable our professional employees to eliminate some of their labor-type activities. Our technicians will be encouraged to accept duties up to the very limit of their capabilities and experience."

Because the full depth and meaning of a purpose cannot be wholly conveyed by the words of charters and mission statements, Kiefer and Stroh (1984) believe it helpful to use the *vision* of a desired future to represent and communicate their purpose. Such a vision statement captures the individual's values and strivings in a way that directs the energy in an organization toward that outcome. The focus on the creative possibilities for attaining the future accomplishment takes people beyond the limitations of what they are doing now and how they do it to planning how to make new and different solutions achievable. A further benefit identified with this positive practice of clarifying purpose and vision is that it catalyzes alignment. "Alignment is the special condition wherein people operate freely and fully as part of a larger whole . . . and consciously assume responsibility for its success" (Kiefer and Stroh, 1984, p. 175). Alignment goes beyond agreement; it seems to also generate commitment based on the shared values and aspirations that have been discussed, explored, refined, and focused on a specific organization result. Kollmorgen Corporation's vision is described as that of a "diamond in the sky," with individuals being facets of its brilliance. Dayton-Hudson envisions itself as the "purchasing agent for its customers," which becomes the basis for a high service orientation throughout the organization. Vision statements such as these are also captured in the similar form that is referred to as a superordinate goal.

In Search of Excellence (Peters and Waterman, 1982), *Managing for Excellence* (Bradford and Cohen, 1984a), and *The Art of Japanese Management* (Pascale and Athos, 1981) have described the value of *superordinate* or *overarching goals*. Such goals go beyond the basic purpose or mission statement to capture the uniqueness in an organization's belief system. That is then applied to its work effort. Such statements are applicable not only at the organizational level but also at the departmental level, where they have the capacity to translate routine activities into purposeful effort. This type of goal fulfills several functions (Bradford and Cohen, 1984a, p. 85-86): (1) It unites and inspires members with a vision that justifies extra effort: "progress is our most important product," "we cure diseases by new medicines," or "to fight inflation by designing equipment that reduces manufacturing costs." (2) It serves as a standard by which to make decisions. (3) It makes clear the direction that the department or organization should strive toward: it defines the future.

In summary, the various alternatives described above can be used as the basis for focusing and directing the organization's energies into the activities that produce results. Upper levels of management have the responsibility to provide guidance and direction to subordinate levels concerning the organization's purpose, its aspirations for future accomplishment, and its beliefs as to how to make that happen through both technical and human processes. We believe that this is best done through a participative process that clarifies values as described in Chapter One and uses the resulting data in defining and setting goals for the technical and human processes.

The first step in this process is setting out the purpose or mission statement: what are we all about? An ongoing difficulty is that it is almost impossible to deal with only one practice at a time, since there is so much interrelationship. For example, it is not at all unusual to discuss the vision while seeking agreement on the mission statement.

Through the natural flow of discussion, or as a second step, we suggest that a manager establish a vision statement or superordinate goal. Because this is a relatively new application area, there is not a precise model to follow. We find that either can be implemented at all levels throughout the organization. The process of exploring ideas and beliefs to develop the vision or superordinate goal is as important as the statement itself. From that view, it is most desirable for managers to involve as broad a group of effected subordinates and staff as possible and practical. Flowing out of—and sometimes with—the organization's vision or superordinate goal will be an effort to define how you might go about creating the alternative future that has been chosen and is being developed as you move toward more traditional planning practices. The flow of this process is level by level: first defining the larger organization's position and expectations, then defining each subordinate group's position, and finally developing each individual's contribution. With a clear mission statement for the larger organization above, each manager at lower levels is able to use that statement as guidance for developing a mission statement reflecting that level's contribution to the whole organization's result. At each level, management has the opportunity to validate the operational effectiveness of needs defined and responses provided. At each level, this same cycle is repeated to keep all subgroups integrated with the organization's purpose.

Once the organization's values have been clarified, an alternative future has been chosen, and direction and guidance have been provided, it is possible to use standard planning techniques to build back from that desired accomplishment. Such an approach is common practice when using netwcrk or systems techniques in planning. This allows us to develop the various strategic choices, organization goals, action plans, and supporting efforts that will be helpful in achieving the result that has been described. Working with the future in this way forces managers to take more responsibility for what they will experience in the future. These are all applied planning techniques that bring planning to the level of meaningful managerial experience. In doing that, they bring everyone into a higher level of involvement in the design of their future, what represents hope for the future, and what behavior, activity, and accomplishment are necessary for attainment of what is clearly understood as being good for both the organization and the individuals within it. In their performance, then, people are doing things that *they* want to do while being aligned with the goals of the organization. This is the richness of positive management practices that provide a highly motivated and fulfilled work force.

With a statement of the vision and purpose, the organization has its primary guidance and direction. It has a reference for validating choices in the decision-making process. Concern now focuses on setting operational goals throughout the organization and getting the commitment of individuals to do what is necessary to achieve them. The role-clarification process presented in the following chapter provides ways to clarify performance expectations and structure task responsibilities so that there is a basis for holding people accountable for accomplishment.

3

Building Commitment
by Clarifying Roles
and Experiences

Have you ever wondered what it is that you are really being held accountable for as a manager? Have your subordinates asked, "What's expected of me?" Have you been told, "That's not in my job description!" when trying to deal with the issue of performance and responsibility? Have you sometimes wondered why some individuals do not seem to understand what the "important" work is and that some things need to be done certain ways? Role clarification is concerned with developing appropriate responses for these questions and expectations.

The previous chapter discussed ways in which managers can create the vision and goal direction that are essential for keeping their organization focused on its desired accomplishment. As a manager, you are also expected to provide the leadership in getting—and keeping—people committed to attainment of that result. In this chapter, you will find some tools to help define what each individual is expected to do and how it should be done in order to maintain a positive organizational climate and commitment.

Defining the expectations surrounding climate and commitment is a basic effort for the implementation of participative management, which Nash (1983) describes as the *one* criterion that differentiates positive climates from negative ones. He also presents this list of climate dimensions identified by the Hay Group, a consulting organization known for its expertise in personnel and compensation: organizational clarity, decision-making structure, organizational integration, management style, performance orientation, organizational vitality, compensation, and human resource development. Role-clarification work is an easy way for the manager to positively explore and resolve the concerns in each of these climate areas.

It is your responsibility as manager to initiate this clarification process, to be actively involved in it, and to provide decisions that are necessary for the appropriate direction and control of the achievement of results. Similarly, as a subordinate, it is equally important that you be involved in the definition of your own performance expectations, that you seek clarity when there is ambiguity, that you accept the responsibilities that are defined and commit yourself to their achievement, and that you are answerable (accountable) for that performance commitment in all respects. While developing understanding and commitment in yourself, your subordinates, and other supporting individuals and groups, you will be managing your organization toward the outcomes described in your vision and goal statements. This maximizes the likelihood of a high-performance work group with clearly defined performance measures for use in managing accountability.

Beyond providing a structured way to implement participative management techniques, role clarification helps individuals to develop their own realization of personal contribution to organization results by working out the details of how they and their work group accomplish it. When developed in depth, role clarification provides subgroups and individuals with organizational direction, task priority and focus, and identity within the larger organization. This gets people involved and invested in their success as part of the organization's performance, which establishes both self-worth and ownership in the achievement. These two are contributions to motivation and a positive perception of the organization's climate.

In *Making MBO/R Work* (Beck and Hillmar, 1976), role

clarification was described as a major part of what we identify as the "navigation system" (see also Chapter Six). *Role* is a term used to refer to any position a person holds in a system (organization), as defined by that person's own expectations and the expectations of other significant persons about that position (Pareek, 1976, p. 211). One's "job role" has been described as "the total *set* of things a worker is expected to *be* (attitudes, values, personality) and to *do* (tasks, functions, responsibilities) in a job" (Bell, 1982, p. 48). Role has also been described (Kuhn and Beam, 1982) as a unit of organization structure in which an individual's defined activities constitute the basic building block for developing the hierarchy presented in an organization chart.

In role clarification, you are seeking to integrate relationships that are necessary for doing a particular job. This will develop clear arrangements and agreements with others on issues such as what tasks or activities need to be performed, and by whom; what accomplishment is expected from those activities; who will make which decisions, and whether any will be made jointly; who will provide what kind of support to whom; to whom things are reported, about what, how often, and in what format; who can tell whom to do what, and under what circumstances; what management style the organization will seek to implement; and how its members will function at the interpersonal level.

Engaging in this type of role-clarification process takes you far beyond the practices usually associated with developing job descriptions, which typically describe a range of activities to be performed. With role work, we develop the understandings, agreements, and expectations that are part of being in a productive human relationship. Through this process, we determine the way a person's or a group's work affects or fits together with the work of others. We develop and negotiate agreements, or "contracts," that do not rely primarily on authority or control but seek to build positive commitment and accountability for being supportive—in an empowering way—through personal relationships. Through this process, people come to know what is included in their jobs and what is expected of them in doing them.

Functional Clarity

You are probably working in some way with the functional aspect of role clarification now. Frequently, this will be expressed in a job description or less formally as, "You know what needs to be done around here, so just make sure it gets done!" In getting started with role work, you need to identify the task activities and boundary conditions necessary for bringing about the desired organizational outcome. Ideally, this process starts at the departmental level—for example, personnel, finance, marketing, engineering, or production—and flows downward through the hierarchy. You can, however, start at any organizational level by making your own assumptions about higher levels and clarifying your own situation.

As a manager seeking to clarify roles, you first establish the organizational role, or purpose, for your group and then develop individual roles. The purpose statement defines the desired accomplishment, or outcome condition, that is expected as a result of the work done by your group—its contribution to the accomplishment of the next, higher level in the organization—and provides guidance for developing internal role statements. The statement will preferably be prepared through some form of group or team process. Because higher levels in the organization have not usually prepared this kind of "input" to work with, we have found that most managers tend to "skip over" the organizational-role work and move quickly to individual roles, which they can engage more comfortably at the activity level. This defeats the purpose of an integrated, level-to-level relationship with a clear basis for organizational contribution and performance accountability.

The translation of group or organization purpose into working roles within the group is sometimes confusing because of the manager's "linking pin" position. The ambiguity has to be clarified by defining whether you, the manager, are looking up or down in the organization. As you look "up" in the organization from any level, you are in the position of a "role" supporting the purpose of that level. Looking downward, you are translating your commitment into an expression of your organization's purpose for subordinate levels to use as their direction in developing their own roles. All these statements need to be expressed in outcome form so that there is clarity about what the group's activities must produce. For example, if you were the manager—chief—of a fire department, your department's functional role (clarification) statement might define its purpose (in outcome terms) as "minimal loss of life and property due to fire." (Looking "up," this is a commitment to the director of public safety's purpose: a safe and secure environment for citizens.) This purpose might be elaborated as follows:

Role Identifier	Outcome Statement
Fire suppression	Fire extinguished with minimal loss
Fire prevention	Fewer fires
Education	Reduced losses
Maintenance	Equipment available when needed

This example illustrates some of the characteristics that managers and work groups have found helpful when they have implemented this form of role clarification. Significant points identified are:

- *Productivity:* The outcome statement provides a basis for knowing specifically what has to be done and defining the priorities. Goals, activities, and performance standards can be clearly focused to produce that outcome.
- *Communications:* The format of the clarification process provides the structure for opening and maintaining dialogue between groups and individuals. During the various explorations, there is a sharing of information, defining of boundaries, and agreement on expectations. This is an opportunity for the manager to establish major communications links and maintain interaction. In the illustration above, for example, the chief has an interest in the shared agreements to be developed by the maintenance and fire-suppression groups to clarify the various work issues described earlier in this chapter.
- *Creative problem solving:* This is a primary opportunity to manage differences toward agreement in a way that seeks to

achieve the fullest use of the available resources in the fulfillment of the desired outcome condition.
- *Human issues:* A wide variety of personal and interpersonal
  concerns can be dealt with to provide balance, ownership,
  and identity with the work situation.

The control or task orientation of most organizations has
not provided most of us with experience in developing role
statements. However, with the increasing acceptance of practices such as these, which are intended to develop a positive
commitment within individuals, we find many managers who
can appreciate the desirability of using such a process but do
not know how to do it and are uncomfortable with experiment-
ing on their own. When it comes to actually doing role-clarification work, there tends to be considerable resistance. The outcome statements, for example, are often discounted as too
simple to be of much value or as being obvious. But this is to
deny the importance of the *process* in which the statements are
developed and used. The organization's outcome statements
plus the supporting data and agreements establish significant
reference points for ongoing guidance, direction, and decisions.
The following is an abbreviated description of a conversation
with a business owner who was trying to develop a better basis
for accountability with his sales manager:

> The owner had been describing his own irri-
> tation about how the salespeople were greeting cus-
> tomers. He stated that he expected his sales man-
> ager to train the salespeople to do what was right
> (a traditional activity- and control-oriented state-
> ment).
> The owner was asked: "How would you
> know they were trained? What would you expect
> the salespeople to do that would tell you the sales
> manager was performing in his role function for
> training? What is it that you will hold him respon-
> sible for?"
> The owner's response focused on the sales-

people's knowledge of technical and functional aspects of the organization's products, the manner in which customers were to be treated, and his desire that the salesperson obtain for the customer "in-house" information necessary for continuing service by the organization through the installation process. One point he emphasized was that customers should be greeted in a way that put them at ease and gave them the feeling of a friendly environment.

"Customers at ease" and "friendly environment" were identified as outcome conditions to be created by the salespeople, for which they can be held accountable, though specific ways of measuring these outcomes would require additional definition.

From this brief example, you can see the opportunities for clarifying a variety of issues and concerns from the owner to the sales manager to the salespeople. The activity definition of "training the salespeople to do what is right" does not provide the clarity of expectations, understanding, commitment, and accountability for organizational performance that would be provided by our practice of exploration, development, and definition through a participative process.

"How to" Techniques

As indicated earlier, *role* is defined by the expectations that individuals have of a given position or organizational function. Our role-clarification approach provides a structure for sharing those expectations through a variety of ongoing discussions between work-group members. This will develop an understanding of expectations, a negotiated agreement to a particular "set," and a commitment to the performance that will fulfill the agreement.

There does not seem to be one all-inclusive role-clarification technique. We have evolved an approach that utilizes a variety of practices to provide a comprehensive coverage of the concerns that we have identified as important. Open discussion and the sharing of ideas and expectations are fundamental to all of these practices as we work with them, though in many cases they could also be implemented in a directive way by the manager doing the developmental work and telling subordinates what is expected of them. There are many variables that affect the definition of role and the relative usefulness of various practices. In general, it is desirable to use as many different practices as possible for the clearest definition of what will constitute expected performance. Each of the practices described could easily stand on its own, but collectively they will enable a work group and its members to develop a comprehensive set of expectations as a basis for performance management. We have already discussed the following practices as basic contributions to role clarification and primary reference points: stating the role's purpose with an outcome description, as in the fire department illustration; defining the functional role identifier with an outcome statement, such as "fire suppression"; and using the outcome statements to draw out additional clarifications concerning who is going to do what and how, as with the owner and sales manager illustration. For purposes of discussion and presentation, these and the following items are considered separately. It is important to realize that, in practice, these items are likely to flow together for consideration without a specific order. The practices to be discussed in the remainder of this chapter are: boundaries, which are important in defining task responsibilities, or "what's mine and what's yours"; task responsibilities at the individual level, which are similar to role identifiers at the group level; issue diagnosis and "getting clear" forms, which are questionnaires that provide a structure for discussing various aspects of the work and environment; responsibility charting, which is another structural tool for helping to define responsibility and authority discussions; and relationship clarification to facilitate definition of and agreement on the nature of the relationships necessary for the accomplishment of the work objectives. The individual and group task-outcome statements and relationship clarification are the two primary efforts in role clarification. The other practices described are supportive techniques that are important for providing additional understanding of the expectations and definition of performance.

In the role-clarification process, we are dealing with these issues (Jones, 1975): *role concept*—a person's view of his or her job and how he or she has learned to do it; *role expectations*—what the boss and others think the job is and how it should be done; *role agreement and acceptance*—what the person is willing to do as a result of the data sharing and negotiating of differences; and *role behavior*—the person's actual performance. The clarification effort can take place between a manager and subordinates individually, or it can be used as a part of a team-building effort. Since there is increasing need to work all the interfaces, the group approach is preferred. The starting point is to develop and share as fully as possible the concepts and expectations that are present in a working group. We have found that this is often difficult for both managers and subordinates, for they have not been expected to be open and accountable with each other in this way. Groups that we work with will usually have done some preparation work to share their values and explore their willingness to work in a participative manner before we come together this way.

As the manager, you will most likely be the first person to clarify your role. You will seek to identify those task activities and relationships that are your contribution to producing the expected outcome. The structured format described below provides the basis for evolving through the interactive process what you, the focal person, are willing to do and accept as your responsibility and commitment to the group and its performance as well as yourself. For those who have not shared and explored in this way before, this can be a growing experience, though it is sometimes also a bit "scary" to open up new relationships with those around you. This book was written to provide some "maps" or understanding of what to expect so that it will not be totally uncharted territory.

Boundaries. What is ours as a group? What is mine; what is yours as individuals? These are some of the concerns that need to be resolved about boundaries, the places where we come into contact with others. In most organizations, there is considerable ambiguity, and often "hassle," because people are unclear about where their functional responsibility—both organizational and individual—starts and stops. Many managers like that condition and will resist any serious effort to get more specific. There are frequent protests about the loss of freedom or control, since most of us like to keep our options open. This is a critical choice point for the manager, since having accountability and responsibility requires clear definitions of major items such as boundaries. Getting clarity between groups at the organizational level can be difficult; however, within working groups, it is always possible to negotiate an appropriate agreement if the differences are managed in a problem-solving way.

Some different types of boundary issues are illustrated in the following examples: In hiring employees, how clear are the boundaries with the personnel function (and perhaps even with your manager) concerning issues such as recruitment, interviewing, selection, and orientation? Would you like to have a different boundary condition in any of those areas? Some boundaries may be based on geography or defined territories, while others are determined by function or technology. The influx of personal computers is creating many fuzzy boundary conditions. When a production or staff unit has such a tool, who is responsible for its maintenance, programming, information accuracy, and security? In working with groups on issues such as these, we find that resolving boundary concerns will free the individuals involved to direct their energies into productive performance instead of fighting "boundary" battles.

Choices you make about the nature of your boundaries will influence the flow of your organizational energy, material, and information. What will be the degree of openness and permeability? How acceptable is it for "outsiders" to enter your group's work area to get information or help? Are people encouraged to reach out across their boundaries? In whatever choices you make here, you are expressing values; we believe these values need to be consistent within the framework of positive practices at the organization outcome level. Thus, if the larger organization is seeking to develop more trust throughout its operations, consistency would suggest that open boundaries and risk taking with others need to be encouraged. Developing closed conditions and being secretive around boundary issues would not be supportive of the organization's direction or beliefs.

Getting clear about boundary issues includes identifying specific responsibilities for coordination and work flow to achieve the desired organization results. It is more helpful and positive to make conscious choices and clearly define such role issues than to let them informally emerge or continue to create confusion, as is the case most of the time. Such functional issues are frequently inseparable from relationship issues and, in practice, must be worked on together. This is especially true in an organization where there is a strong people orientation that demands significant sensitivity to the interaction of both individuals and work groups in a problem-solving way. The discussion of relationship issues in a later section will include additional boundary considerations.

Task Responsibilities. In most organizations, the first point of reference for role work is individual activity. Though that is important information and what we tend to be familiar with, it is not the primary reference for performance accountability. The activity orientation comes mainly from job descriptions, which list things workers are supposed to do for control purposes. But those job descriptions rarely provide any data on specific responsibilities for the accomplishments that should flow from the activities.

In the functional part of role clarification, we are seeking to focus on expressing what is supposed to happen as the result of the activities you do, rather than just listing the activities that you do. The result should be the "driver" for determining that what you are doing is effective. We find that managers tend to prefer to build on what is being done and let that be the justification and driver. In that case, whatever happens must be what is supposed to be. This course of action raises fewer questions and matches most individual's notions of the way management is supposed to work by maintaining a relationship that tends to be oriented toward control (boss) and dependency (subordinate). Opening things up as we are proposing leads to more interaction, sharing of wants, negotiating of differences, and problem solving to maximize what is best for both the organization and the individual. Here, the need is to develop specific statements of working-level expectations and a commitment to appropriate responsibilities and accomplishments within the work group. This is usually done by working down, or back, from the result at the higher level and constantly testing for contribution and appropriate continuity in the relationships.

Issue Diagnosis. We have found the use of several approaches to be helpful for developing the various types of information and interaction that you will want as manager. When these are applied across a period of time, they will build more trust and openness as well as develop a deeper understanding of the individuals and the situation. The values-clarification discussions described in Chapter One are particularly helpful in getting individuals into a more positive, sharing relationship in dealing with their "wants" in the role situation. Harrison (1974) describes an issue diagnosis process that can also be used in role-clarification discussions. In such a diagnostic meeting the focus is always on improving one's own effectiveness. Each person will identify what he or she would like to see the other person (1) do more of or do better, (2) do less of or stop doing, and (3) continue to do because it is particularly helpful for increasing their effectiveness. This approach is simple enough for a manager to use without assistance, though managers often want to have a consultant or trainer present to help them. Ordinarily, the manager will have done some preparatory work with the group to get them ready for working in a more open and participative way in a team-building process such as this. Having established some basis for working together in this manner, the general process would be for a "focal" person, whose role will be clarified, to be designated and for each person to consider his or her relationship to the focal person and what might be changed to make it more effective. In response to the three effectiveness improvement concerns listed above, the data reflecting the group member's "wants" are developed and presented in a group meeting at a designated time. Similarly, the focal person will have been preparing a comparable set of data for each of the individuals involved in the clarification process.

It is difficult to predict the type of item that might be presented as a "want" in these open sessions. It is important for all participants to accept that the answer might be "no." We believe, however, that a significant aspect of the support system is being aware of needs and seeking to satisfy them as fully as possible for each individual.

In a clarification exchange between a manager and subordinates, these were some typical expressions of the subordinate's "I want more of——from you": "I want you to listen to me and my input"; "I want you to tell me what results you want"; "Give me more goal direction"; "Give me more freedom"; "Give me more feedback on how I'm doing"; "I want more true delegation." And "I want less of——": "your telling me how to do my job"; "your control." Similarly, managers have expressed these wants for "more of——": "I need more feedback from you about what's happening"; "I need more 'drive' from you"; "Ask for what you want from me"; "Tell me when there is trouble and what it is about." And "I want less of——": "grumbling over nonessentials"; "your always 'waiting' for something—I want more doing."

In your early sessions, you might not get much response. You will need to provide support, safety, and encouragement to draw out additional helpful sharing. For example, a good communications practice is to provide specific descriptions of behavioral incidents to support and illustrate the basis for your wants and to request the same of others. The true value of sharing the various statements lies in their being the catalyst, or structure, for starting a deeper, meaningful dialogue about what is important for the organization and the individual. We have found that, as the data are shared, it becomes much easier to negotiate—and experience—committed behavior and inspired performance. Such sharing and responding communicate caring and the opportunity to influence things that are important for the individual. This is the practice of managing differences.

The "getting clear" form shown in Exhibit 2 is another general tool to use in role clarification. We often use this form in team building to help groups become aware of the larger system perspectives as well as their own task activities. It helps a group to examine its purpose and whom it is serving as an organization. As a manager, you can work with this form in much the same way as described for issue diagnosis.

Exhibit 2. Clarifying Your Role.

---

1. Identify the primary work groups or individuals with whom you have a working relationship.
2. State your understanding of the desired outcome condition or organization result for your work group.
3. a. What activities or tasks do you think you (the focal person) should be doing to contribute to that outcome?
   b. What specific responsibilities come from those activities or tasks? (Only focal person answer.)
4. What conflicting activity or task expectations for your job are you aware of from others? (Only focal person answer.)
5. List any areas of confusion or ambiguity that you have about what you should be doing in your job.
6. List any areas of confusion or ambiguity that you have about what other members of this team should be doing to accomplish their job function(s).

Once the focal person is designated, the work group responds to the questions from that perspective. In item 1, you will indicate the primary work groups and individuals who are involved in the work group's accomplishment. Item 2 is a statement of the work group's desired outcome condition as the focal person understands it. In practice, this should also be done for the larger system to verify an understanding of its purpose. Item 3 is the statement of the specific tasks or activities to be done by the focal person to contribute to the organization's results. Here, the group should state their detailed expectations of what the focal person should be doing. This is basic information for discussion in the negotiating and clarifying process.

Item 4 is for the focal person only. It should be used for comparison with the input of others as presented in item 3. It is important here to check the match for congruity. If the focal person is aware of expectations that do not match, what has been done to resolve the differences and improve operational effectiveness and team connectedness? Developing clarity here will establish responsibility for specific actions and relationships in maintaining communications and managing differences. Item 5 is answered in terms of what the focal person should be doing. Item 6 should be stated in terms of other members of the work group.

As with issue diagnosis, once each individual has prepared the information, it is shared and clarified for understanding. Using a positive, problem-solving approach, a final position of agreement and acceptance is developed among the various individuals. Any unresolved items must continue to be negotiated toward a final decision and commitment.

Responsibility Charting. This is another technique for getting clarity about a group's work processes. It requires that the manager and the work group analyze and confirm the work flow and the interconnectedness of necessary activities. Identifying specific responsibilities will bring about considerable discussion and sharing of values and perceptions as an existing process is validated or improved. Though the initial focus is on functional responses of groups and individuals, you will find that relationship issues are immediately present as well. When a group does not work with an organization-outcome orientation and test the contribution of each "responsibility," it may be engaging in activities that do not make much contribution to organizational performance.

As described in considerable detail in Beckhard and Harris (1977) and Watson (1981), the mechanics of application are easy and use much of the same information that has been referred to previously. In general, you are working as a performance team to integrate your work efforts and validate the responsibilities for various performance tasks. The agreements flowing from the discussions are presented on a grid format as the "chart of responsibilities." Typically, the chart's left side has a column in which the group's performance responsibilities are listed. When the action focus for that column has been identified, the various groups and individuals necessary for performance are listed across the top, using the remaining columns. Within the matrix thus formed, you can identify the necessary actions with appropriate letters:

> *R*esponsibility to initiate action and ensure that the performance is accomplished.
> *A*pproval by the person who has the right to say "yes" or "no" to actions and requests.
> *S*upport for those providing logistical support and resources for performance.
> *I*nformation about actions that have been taken.

The managers that we have worked with have been amazed by the things that came out in the discussions and the clarity of direction that was available, after their groups had worked through such responsibility-charting experiences. It took considerable discussion and, often, digging for additional detail and understanding of the system, and there were differing forms of resistance to engaging in such an undertaking both before and during the experience. Our strong preference is to start from the organizational or group perspective and define individual work on the basis of contribution and accomplishment. However, many "beginning" groups will start from the individual and build upward, since that is a more familiar orientation.

Your efforts at functional clarity are directed toward getting definitive statements, understanding, agreement, and commitment to the specific task-oriented efforts necessary for productive organizational performance. Through a systematic exploration and definition of the desired performance outcomes, you will have identified appropriate behaviors that will satisfy those performance expectations. These "functional" techniques, however, are just part of the total process we have been working with. The additional aspects of relationship will be considered below in greater detail.

Relationship Clarification

For a variety of reasons, most managers have not been very concerned with developing positive, supportive relationships for carrying out work until recent years. A strong orientation toward efficiency and specialization, along with avoidance or denial of many of the human concerns of employees at work, has led managers to an "either/or" position between functional task concerns and human relationship concerns. With the positive practices presented in this book, we are seeking to facilitate a "both/and" condition in which tasks and relationships are developed in an appropriate balance. We believe it to be increasingly important for managers to acknowledge and accept the significance of relationships for effective performance and to reflect a caring, supportive attitude that individuals at all organizational levels expect as part of the move toward more participation. Positive relationships contribute to inspired organizational performance.

One view of the existing situation is that "role is the armor I wear to keep from knowing you . . . an excuse mechanism that permits me to do what the job requires even though that requirement may conflict with my own values and ethics" (Crockett, 1981, p. 78). Crockett goes on to say, "As a consequence, the relationships are sterile, cold, impersonal, programmed and devoid of human contact." Smith (1982) indicates that the essence of organization is the system of relations that draws the parts of an entity into a whole that is conceptually much more than the mere aggregation of its parts.

The complexity of our growing technology makes it necessary to achieve a level of relationship that we have not achieved in the past. We have been in too many situations where sales was selling one thing, production was building something at variance with what was sold, service had little if any capability to make a "field" modification to make it right, and management had little interest in creating an organizational response system that would bring those functional units together in any integrated way. In fact, management often is unaware of the operational problem, because everybody is reporting that *they* are doing their job the way it is supposed to be done. Developing relationships that are trusting and supportive for organizational performance and productivity is becoming essential.

Issues. Relationships are always concerned with what is happening between people or groups. They have to do with the nature of our response or connection to someone or some group with whom there is a history of interaction and an anticipation of some kind of future. Relationships exist only where there is some form of interdependency. They tie things together for performance.

Building trust in the relationship is a major part of establishing a support system within the work group. We prefer to build that trust through shared goals and the interactive development of task and person responsiveness through role clarification. The technical demands of the work itself represent a "safe" common ground on which to start developing the trust for application in more sensitive areas. Some of the work characteristics that influence relationships are complexity, levels of expertise required and held, human factors versus technology, and the ambiguity involved in the outcome (Cohen and others, 1980). Other influences that have to be explored are the organization's culture, its technology, its reward system, the status of the individuals involved, and personal aspects of each individual.

Application. The role-clarification process provides a structure that helps people try alternative ways of working together. When things are not going right, people know it and want to make it better. Focusing on the desired work accomplishment, they find it easier to negotiate relationship issues and become more productive themselves. You will find in practice that many of the relationship concerns are worked on concurrently with the task-clarification effort, since they are so interdependent. Task issues are generally concerned with the functional or technical "what" of work accomplishment, whereas relationship has to do with the "how" and is often dealt with as part of some other issue, such as management style.

The choice to be more participative provides an illustration of the intertwining of issues that makes relationship clarification rather complex at times. Inherent in participation is an assumption of more openness in work activity, and the relationship discussion about being open is likely to include such questions as: How might we express caring? What do we expect of each other in the area of listening and being supportive? What is likely to happen when we disagree with each other? What are our needs for being included or excluded on various organizational issues? What do we want from each other for professional-level growth? As the manager, you will find it helpful to keep in mind that each work group has its own unique situation. This demands the development of appropriate specifics based on the experiences of the individuals as well as the task and personal expectations that they bring.

Even though the primary focus of role clarification may be on what it takes to be effective in getting our work accomplished, there is also a broad spectrum of relationship concerns that need to be addressed to satisfy various individual needs. These will frequently start from a specific task activity, and the clarification effort has to identify the expectations of each group member and develop a commitment to specific actions or behaviors. A typical list of discussion topics might include:

- Information or input data that I need from you, how often, and in what form.
- The nature of our boundaries, their impact on our relationships, how they structure our relationships, and what might happen if we changed them.
- Assistance I need from you to be able to do my job more effectively and similar peer-level concerns, including trust issues: Will you really help me when I need it?
- Any of the subjects that tie a manager and his or her subordinates or peers together: authority, responsibilities, items to be delegated, work-assignment procedures, meeting schedules, management style, decision making, degree of openness, support expectations, personal and organizational values and ethics, and so on.

There is no absolute listing of possible topics. The most important thing that you can do as manager is to create an open process and environment in which there are freedom and trust to express the issues and concerns that need to be clarified. This is an ongoing process, not something to be done once and remain unchanged. As people change, as situations change, as technology changes, you need to be discussing and adjusting the agreements and expectations. From our own experience, we know that it takes regular attention to being supportive to get and keep the process open. Our own expectation is that managers will provide this form of leadership in those organizations that seek to implement this managerial approach.

To Implement or Not to Implement?

Before implementing role clarification, it would be desirable for you and your work group to discuss and validate some assumptions, such as that some form of a participative style of management is acceptable, that the group is willing to begin functioning with openness, trust, sharing, and support, and that accountability is expected, is accepted, and will be supported. Dependability is a key factor in the implementation of a clarified role. We are seeking clarity about the intention of the relationship and the willingness of both parties to make it work. Two questions to ask yourself regularly when working with role clarification are: "Am I avoiding a responsibility in this situation?" and "Am I avoiding something in this relationship?" Whenever the answer to either is a "yes" or the question is avoided in any manner, you should explore for further awareness with: "Why am I doing that?" or "What is the advantage to me to avoid in this way or in this situation?" Your response will give you the basis for problem solving and a position of greater accountability.

Role clarification is a dynamic change process as well as a way to provide structure to make that change effort a controlled process. It is important that the hope of individuals is not overcome by the fear of losing their freedom in some uncontrolled way. With a positive management orientation, role issues will be resolved so that the work group has clarity of direction through which their energy can move into productive performance for both the organization and the individual. In the next chapter, you will learn ways of working with energy to keep it functioning as a supportive resource for individual and group performance. The presence of positive energy in a work group can lead to a "magical" experience, an exceptional performance.

4

The Performance Difference: Transforming Negative Attitudes into Positive Energy

Managers frequently ask the question, "How can I motivate my people?" Presumably, they want their people to work harder with better results, take more initiative, and have more commitment. What we call motivation is a combination of the individual needs, desires, feelings, or ideas that drive or stimulate from within and the energy, or force, that people put behind them. So managing energy involves motives and the energy they inspire.

A manager using positive practices will generate positive energy—a "provider." The manager who uses external force, trying to impose his or her own motives and values on employees by means of threats, pep talks, and various manipulative tactics, generates negative energy—a "depleter." Recently, a manager of a mining operation was given the task of building a dam at his plant. Traditionally, he would give instructions to each of his workers, and the job would require several days. Using positive practices, he called his group of workers together, told them what he wanted, and asked them to plan how they would build the dam. The dam was built in three hours.

65

The goal was understood, and the workers developed the plan of action to which they were committed. Positive energy was present.

In our viewpoint, then, energy has to do with the vitality and vigor of the organization and its capacity to energize and enhance accomplishment and growth in individuals. Energy is the level of physical and psychic force that enables individuals to accomplish tasks, develop and maintain relationships, and think creatively. Managers have to be aware of the energy potential for both individuals and the organization, for it is a critical factor in an organization's success. As Miller (1977, p. 33) observes in his book *Personal Vitality,* "An organization, by the way it organizes, can dull or enhance the vitality of the individuals who work in it."

Managing Positive and Negative Energy

Positive Energy Can Be Magical. Quarterback John Brodie (Murphy and White, 1978, p. 77-78) of the San Francisco 49ers football team provides some insight into exceptional organizational energy with his description of "times when an entire team will leap up a few notches. Then you feel the tremendous rush of energy across the field. . . . When you have eleven men who know each other very well and have every ounce of their attention—and intention—focused on a common goal, and all their energy flowing in the same direction, this creates a very special concentration of power. Everyone feels it. The people in the stands always feel it and respond to it, whether they have a name for it or not." Bill Russell (Russell and Branch, 1979, p. 155) gives another example of exceptional energy in his remarks about a basketball game: "Every so often a Celtic game would heat up so that it became more than a physical or even mental game, and would be magical." When this happened, he could feel his play rise to a new level. The feeling would surround not only him and his teammates but also the players on the other team and even the referees. He described having chills up and down his spine during these moments.

Positive organizational energy is potent. Like John Brodie's San Francisco 49ers, employees whose manager exhibits positive energy are focused on the present, united, aware, contributing without constraint, listening, supportive, risk taking, and trusting. There is an atmosphere full of hope and confidence in the group's ability to solve whatever problems may arise. Emerging solutions move beyond individual ownership. Rather, they reflect the abilities and contributions of group members.

As mentioned above, positive energy is a provider. It provides for hopefulness, helpfulness, and powerfulness and enables people to see possibilities and choices and to be open to change. This leads to the confidence that they can solve problems and the willingness and ability to cooperate and use their power for the organization.

Negative Energy Is Draining. Most individuals are not consciously negative. Being angry, blaming others, and attacking people personally do not make for a comfortable posture. However, when negative energy is present in the organization— energy that is not in accord with the primary thrust of the organization or that creates low self-worth within the individual— individuals tend to respond by exhibiting negative behaviors. There may be arguments with tempers flaring, people pounding on the table, and doors slamming. Confrontation may take the form of blaming and complaining rather than dealing with broken agreements or unsatisfactory performance. This energy is seldom perceived as negative in terms of absolute, either/or positions; rather, it is very situational, based on existing norms within the organization.

Negative energy is a depleter, causing hopelessness, helplessness, and powerlessness. With negative energy, people see no possibilities or choices; they are resistant to change and use their energy against the manager and the organization. Negative energy is soon exhausted, leaving little or no energy at all. Negative attitudes and behaviors tend to feed on themselves and stimulate more negativity. Judgmental and punitive behavior are prevalent, and people feel out of control. Statements such as "Things will never change" or "You just can't win" indicate the level of despair associated with negative energy. While the ex-

citement around anger and hostility may be intense, it is coun-
terproductive and fosters poor problem-solving efforts.

Organizations experiencing negative energy are frequently faced with poor employee performance. Energy is expended
on attacking individuals, avoidance, anger, and punitive action,
at the expense of promoting exceptional positive performance.
When people's positive energies are absorbed or neutralized by
such reactions, they are not available for problem solving. Low
trust levels prevail, and there is little risk taking. Individuals
seem to do the minimum, because it is safe and in keeping with
the energy available to do the job. An example of negative
energy leading to passivity was the publisher who resisted
change and chastised anyone suggesting change, even though ad-
vertising revenues and circulation were declining steadily. Those
employees with positive energy soon left; those who stayed did
the minimum and avoided the president. The decline acceler-
ated, and bankruptcy and liquidation resulted.

Polarity: The Choice Is Yours. There are both positive
and negative aspects—polarity—in every situation and in each of
us individually. Just as a battery or electrical circuit must be
connected and balanced for the energy to flow appropriately
into action, there are some patterns of energy flow in organizations that are important for managers to use for effectiveness in
organizational performance. The awareness of such principles
enables you to recognize and use both positives and negatives in
daily activities. When you emphasize one of these energy points
at the expense of the other, you may lose your desired balance
unless you are integrated into the system. For example, negative feedback can be used in amplifier circuits in a very structured and useful way. When managers choose to use feedback,
they are likely to get a lot of negative energy flow, which must
be integrated into the larger system and transformed into a positive system response. If such negative energy is cut off, ignored,
or unconnected, the system (organization) potential may be lost
or significantly reduced. Even worse is the possibility that the
internal circuits might overload and burn out some resistors,
causing a short circuit in the system. Those who have experienced an electrical short circuit know that it creates quite an

acrid odor; a similarly unpleasant atmosphere might be experienced in organizations whose energy has been severely out of balance.

When both the positive and negative energy are recognized and used appropriately, we are connected and maximizing our energy flow (the voltage, or "juice"). The positive will be the primary consideration for the proper release, flow, and use of our organizational energy. Significant energy, individual and collective, will be available for problem solving, creativity, innovation, and work or task performance.

These electrical analogies give you a framework for examining the attributes and use of positive and negative polarity. They do not determine the individual's or the organization's energy orientation. That is a conscious individual choice concerning behavior and practices. What condition exists as a result of the choices now being made in your situation? Our work with organizations over the last decade has convinced us that the increased vitality and effective performance usually found with the positive polarity make that mode of operation significantly more desirable. Thus, the skill to transform negative energy to positive is highly valued.

Power of Transformation. Individuals and organizations have great powers of transformation. Understanding these powers and their application is helpful in the examination of negative and positive energy. Huxley (1963) describes human beings as the most prodigious transformers within the known universe. As physical transformers, human beings turn air, water, and food into blood, muscle, viscera, and bone. As intellectual transformers, we take ideas, information, and opinions from others and convert them into our own thoughts, personality, and actions.

Human beings are emotional chameleons. Envy and hatred, feelings that are regarded as evil, are transformed into the more acceptable feelings of righteous indignation and moral disapproval. Likewise, guilt can become caution at one extreme or aggressiveness at the other. Being victimized by injustice can produce revenge or a sense of inferiority. Under stress, individuals frequently transform feelings into physical manifestations, such as absenteeism, psychosomatic illness, ulcers, substance abuse, or heart attacks. Awareness of these transformations gives us power to redirect the negative orientation into the positive. This awareness also permits individuals to become voluntary transformers of positive energy instead of involuntary victims of the negative.

Managerial Transformation Techniques

Transformation takes practice, and we must learn to use tools and techniques available to us. Robert Goulding suggests an awareness exercise that is useful in transforming negative energy into positive (Wagner, 1981, p. 74) (we have found that doing this with your eyes closed is often more helpful): Take thirty seconds to think about a negative experience that you have had. Re-experience those feelings. Now take another thirty seconds to reflect on a very pleasant experience that you have had. Re-experience those feelings. What did you find out? You may have demonstrated that you can create your own feelings, both pleasant and unpleasant. If you were unsuccessful the first time, repeat the exercise until you are able to truly experience both pleasant and unpleasant feelings. Know that you can refocus and change your unpleasant or negative feelings to positive feelings in less than a minute any time you wish. The attitudinal choice is yours.

When managers are aware of their power of transformation, they will examine policies, systems, and norms to determine what is required to change from negative to positive. Informal taboos such as "Don't argue with the boss" or "Keep a low profile" are indicators of negativity. These negative norms can be transformed into positive ones by a conscious choice to eliminate them and a focus on the development of a more positive environment that encourages communication and appropriate risk taking.

There are numerous strategies that managers and management groups can use to transform negative thoughts and feelings into positive ones. Some specific techniques are modeling positive behavior; acknowledging the existence of negativity; looking for and identifying the positives in all situations; refraining from collusion on negativity; giving positive recognition (strokes) often; stopping negative games; refraining from using "put-downs"; and using positive verbal communication and clearly stating expectations of each other.

Model Positive Behavior. A manager's positive behavior maintains and develops positive energy. His or her dealings with others are best when they come from a positive frame of mind. The manager is modeling positive behavior when he or she relates to others using a Theory Y (McGregor, 1960) set of assumptions, expecting a lot from people, supporting them, holding them accountable, confronting them, and above all being clear and honest with them without damaging their self-esteem. This positive orientation needs to permeate the organization and be articulated in its goals and values. A manager can demonstrate this by the way he or she talks to employees. Comments such as "I know you can do that job" or "I want you to work on improving your skills this year—how can I help you?" are far better than comments such as "That was a dumb thing to do" or "Why can't you be like Sally?"

Acknowledge Negativity. If an employee complains or criticizes the organization, do not deny it, ignore it, or put the employee down with statements such as "You shouldn't feel that way" or "That's a dumb way to look at things." As a manager, accept that condition as reality for the individual and look for the cause or grievance that is behind this negative behavior. Statements or questions such as "I understand how you feel; what would you like to do about this problem?" or "What would you like from me?" are supportive and introduce the possibility for change. Until you know what is behind the complaining, you have no opportunity to solve the problem. You also have to be open to the fact that the complaint may be a legitimate one on which you should take action.

Another way that a manager can acknowledge negativity is to ask the question "What is the worst thing that can happen in this situation?" After listing the answers to this question, ask "What are the best things that can happen in this situation?" Verbalizing negatives frequently diminishes the reality and severity of fears. On the other hand, the listing of "best things" often provides cues for focusing the transformation process on positive outcomes, generating positive energy.

Look for Positives. Although the search may be arduous, especially in organizations whose employees have negative attitudes, a manager should look for the positives. One approach is to consciously select and express thoughts that are positively oriented. For example, if you, the manager, find that the ideas being presented are all negative or are focused on why something will not work, turn the process around and list all the good points and reasons why it will work. The attitude that things will work out well is helpful.

Quick rejection is stifling. To promote the flow of ideas, consider the positives before the negatives. This technique works especially well with employees who are frustrated with their jobs or angry with a situation in their organization. When the manager gets them to examine the positives and negatives, they often realize that they are causing some of the negatives. With this awareness, the employees can work on changing those negatives over which they have control and create a more positive environment.

Refrain from Collusion on Negativity. Getting caught up in "bitching" or "ain't it awful!" conversations is easy to do. People seem to be attracted to "bad-mouthing" as they are to sensational news stories, and, with each repetition, the negative aspects of the situation tend to get worse. When faced with conversations of this type, the manager must refrain from collusion. Rather, confront the individual by asking: "What do you want to do about this situation?" If the response is "nothing," let go of your involvement and suggest that the other person let go of it also and quit making him- or herself feel bad. However, if the initiator wants to take positive action, assistance should be offered and, if possible, strategies developed to alleviate the situation.

Other strategies for dealing with negative conversations are commenting on the negative aspects and changing the subject to a more pleasant one; asking what can be done to improve the situation or what the positives are in the situation; and laughing at the negativity. If these strategies fail and negativity persists, inform the other person that you do not wish to engage in repeated negative conversations, and avoid excessive contact. When interaction is necessary, the conversation should be focused on the positive aspects of the situation, with little opportunity for discussion of the negatives.

Give Positive Recognition. People need positive recognition! Providing positive recognition, or "strokes," is probably the most significant strategy to establish and maintain positive energy. Such recognition should be given even when people are doing their routine work, "what they are paid to do." Managers frequently resist providing recognition for anything less than exceptional performance. As soon as a manager is aware of good performance or behavior, positive recognition needs to be given, spontaneously and without contingencies or restrictions. You will get the behavior that you stroke. If you are giving only negative feedback, by criticizing or reprimanding, you will get more negative behavior. If you are complimenting people on their performance or behavior, you will get more of that. People cannot stand being ignored. This starts at an early age. If children do not get positive strokes on their behavior or nurturing of their being, they will "act out" and become a discipline problem to force strokes. Negative strokes are better than none at all.

It is well to be aware that there are conditional and unconditional strokes. Conditional strokes are for behavior or performance: "That was an excellent report you gave me yesterday," or "Thank you for the assistance you gave me on the XYZ project. It was most helpful." An unconditional stroke is on the person as a human being. For example, a manager may say, "It's a joy having you here," or "I really like you as a person. It is fun working with you." The most powerful unconditional stroke is touch. A manager who is comfortable giving touch strokes might touch the recipient on the hand, arm, or shoulder when talking with him or her. Of course, the manager must be certain that the other person is comfortable receiving the touch stroke.

Positive strokes must be honest and genuine and given

without expecting anything in return. If there is a manipulative intent, they are phony and harmful, and this will be perceived by the recipient. They are also more effective when given spontaneously. This is one of the most effective tools that a manager has at his or her command. It is motivating and energizing as well as an effective way for a manager to communicate expectations to subordinates.

Stop Negative Games. When negative games are played by managers, there are hidden agendas that tend to reinforce negative attitudes. In the process, people get hurt, and the real problems go unresolved. Boredom and an unresponsive organizational environment promote psychological game playing. Individuals participate to gain recognition and excitement. It is important for managers to be aware of their own negative games (Morrison and O'Hearne, 1977), as well as those of others. One often-played game is "yes, but." A "yes, but" game may be started by a supervisor saying, "I cannot get my employees motivated to get more training." Rather than giving this supervisor advice and solutions to which he or she could respond "yes, but . . . ," we suggest that a manager give a confrontive reply, such as "That can be difficult. What do you plan to do?" or "Is there something you would like me to do to help you?" Such a response forces the supervisor to focus on his or her responsibility for action and the factual data of the situation. Game playing is blocked because problem solving is promoted.

Another psychological game often played by managers is "blemish." A manager playing the game of blemish will always find something wrong with whatever a subordinate does; for instance, "You did a great job, but . . ." or "This is a good report, but you handled the second section poorly by not checking out all the details." If the concern is minor, it might not be necessary to comment on it. When you choose to comment, it would be more positive to replace the *but* with *and*. A more supportive feedback statement would be "This is a good report, and I would like for you to take another look at the second section to see if you can develop more detail in it." A *but* after the positive erases what preceded it in the recipient's mind, and he or she hears only the negative.

Refrain from Using "Put-Downs." Negative words such as *idiot, dummy, fool, inept, jerk,* and *loser* are demeaning and damaging to a person's self-esteem. To maintain a positive environment, a manager should focus on performance or behavior rather than personality. A negative statement would be "Joe, that was a stupid decision you made yesterday. You know better than that." A better statement would be "Joe, let's take a look at how you handled that complaint yesterday. How might you have handled it differently?" A belittling statement is "When you have more experience, Mary, you'll be able to understand what I mean." A positive statement would be "Mary, I don't think I have been clear with you on what I expect. I would like to go over this again with you." Another way: "Was there something you needed on that job that you did not get?" "Killer phrases," such as "we tried that years ago," "we don't do it that way here," and "sounds like too much hassle," are also promoters of negativity. A manager can avoid this by asking people for the facts to support their observations or conclusions.

Use Positive Communication. Honest, straightforward communication is the key to creating and maintaining positive energy. An example of positive verbal communication is asking for what you want from others and expecting them to do the same with you. When managers, subordinates, and peers ask each other for what they want, role relationships are clear and more productive. However, when people suppress their wants, they will experience frustrations and diminished energy. The satisfaction of wants is highly energizing. When we ask for what we want, we will get it most of the time. For instance, a manager might say to her boss: "I want you to support me when I take disciplinary action on my supervisor," "I want you to let me know when I am not performing up to your expectations as soon after an incident as possible," or "I want thirty minutes of your time to discuss the ABC account."

Speaking from the "I" is another example of positive communication. Each of us is an authority on ourselves in that we know what we are thinking, feeling, hearing, and seeing at all times. When you, the manager, start your sentences with "I," other people are clear on where you stand and are able to deal with you in a positive, straight manner, without being defensive. When confronting, start your sentences with "I," never "you," as that can come across as blaming and put the other person on the defensive. Avoid using "they," "someone," "everybody," "people," and so on. Using "I" is specific.

A manager can encourage straight communications by asking who "they," "someone," or "everybody" are. You should also avoid using "we" unless you are speaking for the organization or the group you are representing has given you permission to speak for them. An example of the misuse of "we": In a group meeting, Mary said, "We are not being straight with each other." The "we" needs to be clarified immediately. Is it Mary, or one or two specific people? If this is not clarified, there will be a negative cloud over the group, and the group's problem solving will be blocked.

Be willing to say "no." For a free flow of energy in the organization or a relationship, it is essential that people feel free to say "no" or disagree constructively in a problem-solving way. When people feel free to explore the negative, they are then able to explore the positive more fully. They will be able to say "yes" clearly and be committed to it. Unfortunately, in some organizations, it is a norm that you do not say "no" or disagree with certain people. When this condition exists, the full value of the human resources is not being utilized, and the quality of decisions is likely to be less than it could be.

Not only is it necessary to be able and willing to say "no," but it is also essential that managers are willing to accept "no" from others without feeling that it is insubordination. The "no" can be softened somewhat by giving the reason for the negative response. Of course, when you say "no" to your boss, you are careful about the way that you express it. For instance, a statement may be: "I don't think I should take on this assignment because . . . ," or "I am afraid if I do this job, we will get into trouble." The willingness of a subordinate to disagree with the boss and give the reasons why may be the most supportive thing that the subordinate can do—much better than agreeing just because he is the boss and letting him get into trouble that could have been avoided. Of course, when a subordinate disagrees with the manager's decision, he or she has to accept the final decision and support it even though disagreeing with it. The manager may handle the disagreement as follows: "I understand your position and appreciate your giving it to me. I think it best for the organization that we go in the other direction, and I want you to support this position. I do appreciate your willingness to disagree with me."

Ask open-ended questions. Questions starting with "Why don't you . . . ?", "Why did you . . . ?", or "Don't you think that . . . ?" are closed questions and usually communicate "control" and, possibly, manipulation to get a desired answer. These control-type questions can cause feelings of guilt and self-doubt in the recipient and may lead to angry, fearful, or defensive responses. Open questions are phrased in such a way that the recipient has an opportunity to choose what and how to respond. They begin with who, what, where, when, and how. Open questions will build trust and self-confidence. "Why didn't you follow my instructions?" is a negative way of asking a question. A positive approach would be "Brian, something went wrong this morning. Can you describe what happened?" The latter approach opens the situation for problem solving (Maidment, 1983). Sometimes managers ask questions when they really want to make a statement, such as asking "Don't you think it would be a good idea for me to become more involved in planning the XYZ project?" When what is really being expressed is "I want to be more actively involved in planning the XYZ project."

Be specific and clear. Some ways for a manager to do this are to:

1. Talk directly to an individual in a specific way ("Mary, I don't think you are doing your part. I would like for you to attend these meetings on time and let me know when you are unable to complete an assignment on time.") instead of "broadcasting" to an undefined group ("Some members of this team are not doing their part.").
2. Say what you mean and endeavor to speak in clear, crisp,

and simple sentences rather than paragraphs. Avoid repeating and overexplaining, since these minimize the impact of your message. A manager may handle this by saying, "I am not clear on your point. Would you summarize what you just said in one sentence?"

3. Avoid telling others what they should do: "Sheila, you should listen while I'm talking." A better statement would be: "I feel annoyed when you read while I am talking, Sheila, because I must now repeat everything."

4. Avoid exaggerating words such as *everybody*, *nobody*, *always*, and *never*.

5. Avoid self-imposed constraints, such as saying "I can't" when you really mean "I won't." A test for this is to ask yourself who or what is stopping you after you have said "I can't." When you realize that you are really saying "I won't," you have taken responsibility for your choice and are in a better position to determine whether you want to take action or not.

Establishing Supportive Norms

To effectively transform negative energy to positive energy on a daily basis, it is necessary for the culture of the organization to support this desired change. To change the culture, managers have to look at the existing norms, both formal and informal. Norms are expected behavior patterns and are quite influential. They contribute greatly to the character of the organization.

A manager has to determine whether the existing norms support or are barriers to the positive behavior desired. Where norms serve as barriers, managers have to make a deliberate effort to change them to norms that support the desired new condition. For instance, if the existing norm is to avoid confrontation, managers will have to work to make confrontation a way of life in the organization and a norm that is both expected and rewarded. Some of the areas in which norms will have to be examined are discussed in the next chapter.

✕✕ 5 ✕✕

Changing
Destructive Cultural Norms
into Constructive Ones

✕✕ ✕✕ ✕✕ ✕✕ ✕✕ ✕✕ ✕✕ ✕✕

The examples of cultural norms in the previous chapter point out the manager's need to be aware of the norms, both explicit and implicit, existing in the organization. If these norms are positive, they are supportive of the organization's goals and objectives. These are norms that support hard work, loyalty, quality consciousness, and concern for customer satisfaction. Negative norms are those that have the opposite effect: they promote behavior that works against the organization's achievement of its objectives. Some examples of negative norms are those that sanction "bad-mouthing" the organization, low or limited productivity, absenteeism, theft, secrecy, and "every man for himself."

This chapter will give you, the manager, ways to diagnose the norms in your organization. You will also learn how to change norms to those that are supportive of organizational effectiveness and the behavior you desire. While support from top management is the best way to change organizational norms, each manager can affect the norms in the area over which he or she has control. Individual managers can have considerable influence on their areas—and possibly the total organization—through the use of support groups, described in detail later.

Definition of Norms

In any organizational setting, there are a variety of be-
havioral-level forces at work that influence the organization's
effectiveness and workers' job satisfaction. They are the expected, accepted, and supportive ways of behaving that determine so much of what we do. A person breaking a cultural
norm is usually penalized for it. An example is the manager who
did not keep "fat" in his budget to withstand cuts from upper
management. As a result of his belief in a "bare-bones" budget,
he suffered when there was an across-the-board cut; the manager who went with the norm and padded her figures did not
suffer from the cut. Another example is a new worker on the
production floor, where the workers have established a production norm. When the new worker produces more than her co-
workers, she is soon informed of the production norm and told
to "get with it." If she persists in the greater production, she
will be ostracized and possibly suffer damage to her car on the
parking lot. By supporting normative behavior, groups can influence members to do things that are contrary to their personal
value systems.

Managers have found that when new concepts such as
management by objectives for results (MBO/R), organization
development (OD), and quality circles are implemented, the initial desire and enthusiasm for the new way gradually dwindle
and disappear if the existing norms are not supportive. If management implements the MBO/R concept and everyone works
on achieving their objectives, but the decisions about raises are
based on other criteria, ignoring or downplaying the achievement of objectives, employees receive the message that MBO/R
is not all that important and will concentrate in the future on
what they are rewarded for doing, which might be looking busy,
agreeing with the boss, socializing with the right people, or not
making waves. Another example is the manager who says that
he wants employees to confront each other when there is nonperformance or broken agreements but, when one of his employees confronts him on a broken agreement, becomes angry
and defensive and chastises the employee. In this situation, the

manager is not modeling the behavior that he says he wants. The employees will follow the behavior model of the manager after incidents of this type.

Norms quite often are implicit and not articulated. Allen and Dyer (1980, p. 192) refer to an "organizational unconscious" that "represents those patterns of social behaviors and normative expectations that become characteristics of organizational functioning without the members of the organization consciously choosing the behaviors in question." Individuals may be following norms that have long since outlived their usefulness. For example, they may find it commonplace to be critical of each other and avoid confronting each other and airing their problems, assuming that this behavior is human nature. When a norm of this type has existed for many years, there is a vested emotional interest in maintaining a relatively comfortable equilibrium by letting the sleeping dog lie. For this reason, it is essential for the manager to identify these norms and develop objectives with employees to change those that are limiting the effectiveness of the organization.

Identification of Cultural Norms

The first step is to identify existing norms and determine whether they are positive or negative. This can be done by asking the right questions of people who experience the negative effects of dysfunctional norms, either through questionnaires or by personal interviews. We recommend a combination of the two, administered by a third party to preserve anonymity. Some questions that might be asked in an interview are: "How does one get attention around here?" "How do you say 'no' in this organization?" "What happens when a mistake is made?" "How is strong disagreement handled here?" "When things get rough around here, how do people act?" A questionnaire might ask employees to indicate their agreement or disagreement with statements such as "It's a norm around here: (1) for people to feel responsible for doing their job right; (2) for people to have some input on decisions that affect their work; (3) for people to feel that their work is important." Sample questionnaires are presented in *The Organizational Unconscious* (Allen and Kraft, 1982) and "Organizational Norms Questionnaire" (Alexander, 1978). There are many other similar instruments available.

Before administering a normative survey, a manager should be clear about the objective—what he or she wants to change and how the data will be used to achieve that change. There has to be a commitment to using the answers from employees, because the act of asking the questions raises expectations that things will change; if the survey data are not used, hostility and hopelessness may result. The manager should validate the survey results with employees. They can then develop objectives to change the negative areas and barriers to effectiveness. The survey results should be categorized under areas such as leadership, behavior, group involvement, candor/openness, performance, innovation/creativity, and so forth. They should provide responses to two issues: (1) the way it is now and (2) the way they would like it to be. This identifies the gap that needs to be closed to bring the norms to the desired state.

We recommend an approach similar to the four-step process described in *Beat the System!* (Allen and Kraft, 1980): (1) analyzing the existing state and determining desired change; (2) introducing the desired culture, enabling people at all levels to experience the desired culture and to plan change; (3) implementing the desired culture through individuals, leadership, and group development and organizational programs, policies, and procedures; (4) sustaining the desired culture through recognition, renewal, modification, and extension of the desired culture. The key to achieving the desired change is involvement of employees in the total program so that there is commitment to the new norms. The manager will find that there are some things that can be changed immediately; others may require more time, with action plans, checkpoints, resource support, and accountability. If the manager denies the data, keeps them secret because they are embarrassing, or "massages" them to death by continued discussion without any decision for action, the process will be sabotaged. These diagnostic surveys are best administered in a total organizational effort that is supported by top management, although in a semiautonomous unit, such as a plant or regional office removed from central headquarters, it is best to stay away from questions over which the manager has no control, such as benefits, organizational policies, and so on.

What the Manager Can Do to Change Norms

Each manager can and should take action to change norms that are obviously negative and adversely affect the performance of his or her unit. As mentioned earlier, one of the first steps is to sit down with employees and go over the data from the survey or interviews to validate them. The discussion should get to specifics to facilitate the development of strategies in the most critical areas. In developing the action plans on each objective, the group will identify the barriers to be overcome and the resources that will be needed and clarify who will do what by when. This will include both things that the manager will do personally and things that others will do; it will involve changes to be made in some systems, the way people work together and communicate with each other, the way decisions are made, and training that will be needed.

A change such as meeting more often can be implemented immediately. A change in the way decisions are made can also be made promptly, after some discussion. A change in the salary system may be needed, to give managers more freedom to reward productive behavior. To change a salary system requires considerable study and research and probably will be beyond the province of individual managers. However, they may suggest to top management the need for a more flexible salary system that rewards the top producers. Managers may also find that they have the freedom to administer the existing salary system in ways that recognize excellent performance.

Many changes will require managers to do some deep soul-searching to change their behavior. This may come slowly and painfully, but it is essential to the change process. Clarkson's (1982) experience at Graphic Controls is an example of why patience and perseverance are necessary. In deciding to change his style of management in the early seventies, he agreed to confront the conflict between the way he wanted to function and the way in which his subordinates perceived his leadership. He did this by (1) openly admitting the need for change and professional growth, (2) being willing to modify his leadership methods by using experience-based learning, and (3) committing himself to a management style that developed mutual trust and collaborative teamwork with subordinates. To accomplish this change in behavior, he stated, chief executive officers need the following interpersonal competence skills: (1) to give ownership to their own ideas and feelings and assist others in doing the same, (2) to confront difficult issues with positive attitudes and results, (3) to understand their own actions, behaviors, and their impact on others, and (4) to seek, receive, and effectively manage feedback themselves in order to continue their professional and personal growth. He found that at times this was painful and difficult for his ego to handle. His perseverance in this endeavor paid off in a highly effective organization with a high level of personal satisfaction.

Areas of Change

Some of the normative areas that a manager may have to change are rewards, modeled behavior, confrontation, communication, training, resource allocation, interaction and relationships, orientation, leadership and supervision, innovation and creativity, and humanness.

Rewards. In addition to doing everything possible to disburse monetary rewards to top performers, the manager should use the rewards of recognition, status, praise, special privileges, special projects, and special development. Rewards are in the eyes of the beholder; money is only one reward, often not the most important for many people. A manager using positive practices will distribute the rewards in his or her system to the top performers and those supportive of the positive environment he or she desires. Norms that are barriers exist when the rewards are given to people who do not use positive practices and when those who do use them are punished, for instance, when a manager who disagrees with the boss is met with anger and defensiveness and is later punished, whereas those who always agree with the boss are rewarded. This is the single most powerful normative area for reinforcing the desired positive behaviors.

Modeled Behavior. Managers have the responsibility to model the behavior and the values that they say they want in the organization. To do otherwise sends mixed messages ("Don't do what I do, do what I say.") and causes confusion that will result in negative attitudes. We know that employees tend to follow the boss's lead in behavior, regardless of what is said. The tone of voice and nonverbal behavior send a much stronger message than the words. People are more highly motivated when they see the positive behavior and values modeled by their manager. If a manager says, "I want teamwork," but her subordinates see her in a constant struggle with her associates, little teamwork is modeled, and, therefore, little teamwork will prevail in practice.

Confrontation. Norms of confrontation are supportive when people confront each other as a matter of course as soon as possible after unsatisfactory performance or broken agreements or after someone has done something that has caused problems for other individuals or departments. The norms are not supportive when confrontation is avoided or handled in a destructive manner. A manager who is abusive and attacks a person's self-esteem instead of limiting the confrontation to performance and behavior is confronting destructively. It is also destructive to avoid a confrontation and to suddenly unload months of incidents at one time. The employee should be given the opportunity to correct unsatisfactory performance that may have been unrecognized or forgotten.

Communication. The most frequent comment that we hear in diagnosing management problems is: "We don't communicate with each other." A manager should let employees know what is going on at all times. Regularly talking to people while circulating through the work area and holding regular meetings with the entire work force are two ways a manager can take care of communication problems. For their own security reasons, people need to know the larger picture, as well as the information that is necessary for them to effectively carry out their duties. One company improved productivity further merely by giving employees information on the productivity gains they had already achieved. Another cut absenteeism by 10 percent by writing congratulatory letters to all who had not missed work during the preceding year. Norms of communication are supportive of a positive environment and positive behavior when people communicate with each other in a straight and honest manner. These norms are not supportive when people do not get the information they need to do their job and are not given permission to ask for information when they need it or when some individuals deliberately withhold needed information from others. Such negative norms prevent the flow of positive energy and promote the use of energy in negative behaviors. When a manager refuses to allow an employee to go to another department for needed information, he or she is blocking communication. The reverse of this may exist when one department refuses to give needed information to another department. These actions promote such negative behavior as blaming, criticizing, and destructive competition resulting in duplicated work, poor work relationships, and often political infighting.

Training. One of the finest compliments a manager can give to employees is to see that they get the training they need to do their job effectively and prepare to move up in the organization, if that is their goal. Personally participating in training is another way that a manager can give employees the strong message that the training is important and results are expected. An added advantage of such participation is that each is receiving the same ideas and concepts and can discuss how they can use them in their unit. It also eliminates the complaints of many trainees: "My boss should be here" or "My manager needs this more than I." The trainers should exhibit positive practices and values themselves in their teaching and see that the norms supportive of a positive environment are evident in the training programs. When the trainers are negative, complaining and blaming and showing low energy and little enthusiasm, training is not supportive of positive behavior. Managers should expect their employees to come back from training events with a positive attitude and the skills and knowledge provided by the training.

Training is not supportive when it is looked on as a waste of time and positive results are not expected. Managers should hold training accountable for meeting the objectives of the program and instilling in people a positive attitude.

Resource Allocation. A manager has the responsibility to support subordinates with the resources (personnel, material, and financial) that they need to perform their jobs. For instance, if a manager wishes to change the norms in an organization, he or she will have to commit the necessary time and money for training, conducting attitude and normative surveys, and obtaining the help of consultants. This may necessitate a change if resources have traditionally been allocated to certain favorite people or projects or on a political basis of who knows whom best. When a manager supports his or her employees with adequate resources, those employees are energized and motivated. This commitment has to be ongoing; there has to be a provision for follow-up and renewal each year. It is a never-ending endeavor.

Interaction and Relationships. To support a positive environment, managers must encourage interaction among their subordinates and other units and value the building of productive relationships. They should emphasize the importance of employees building the relationships with other people or units that are necessary for effectiveness in their jobs. Managers themselves must model this behavior and establish it as a norm for the organization. A positive environment is not fostered when there is little or no interaction and relationships are not valued. In some organizations, people seldom talk to each other, and when they do they must be careful of what they say, as it might be used against them. Under such circumstances, people are not willing to help others, and there is a low level of trust and little cooperation. People want to be treated as human beings, not as objects or pieces of furniture. A manager will have fewer problems with employees when he or she interacts with them and builds their self-esteem instead of attacking them with such words as *dumb* or *stupid.* In attacking a person's self-esteem, you are tearing down self-confidence, resulting in lower-quality work and less risk taking.

Orientation. When a new person comes into the organization, the manager must be sure that the desired norms for the unit are communicated. The manager can do this by spending time with the employee during the first few months and seeing that he or she works with employees who support and model the desired norms. Unfortunately, new employees are often put with negative persons and low performers, as they usually have more time available. The manager should see that there is some formality to the orientation procedure to be sure that the positive practices are emphasized and modeled.

Leadership and Supervision. A manager can demonstrate leadership through commitment to change by modeling the behavior desired, seeking out the opinion of subordinates, getting together regularly with the work team to set goals, being constructive and helpful when errors and mistakes are made, involving people directly in the development of changes that affect them, having a clear and consistent way to measure results, and expecting a lot from employees while holding them accountable for improvement.

Innovation. Providing an atmosphere for people to innovate and use their creativity is particularly important in our changing society. A manager has the responsibility not only to be open to innovation but also to expect it and reward it. Historically, many of our organizations have clung to the past, maintaining the status quo. This is an easy way to go out of business today. A manager's attitude toward innovation is crucial to effective management. The manager who resists new ideas, does not give feedback on suggestions, or puts people down for bringing up new ideas is sending employees the message "don't think," or "your ideas are not good." These messages are demeaning and will result in negative behavior and apathy. Concepts such as quality circles are structured approaches to getting suggestions from employees. These fail when managers do not use these suggestions or give feedback on why they cannot use them. When a work group is committed to their idea, they will put forth the effort to make it work. However, they often have less commitment to management's new ideas, even though the ideas may be better. The workers may sabotage management's ideas consciously or unconsciously, with such comments as "It was not my idea," or "I could have told them it would not work." A manager should be aware that one of the finest compliments that he or she can pay a person is to use that person's idea and support it with resources. The reward to the individual or group is personal fulfillment from seeing the idea work and contribute to the effectiveness of the organization.

Humanness. We have mentioned humanness in other normative areas. Managers are being human when they accept themselves and others as human beings and treat others accordingly; when they are aware of differences, see them as assets, and use them accordingly; and when they feel free to compliment others on both their performance and their persons as human beings.

As shown in the normative areas described above, influences and interrelationships overlap. What is modeled is communicated; what is communicated is recognized; and recognition is a form of reward. Though these norms overlap and blend together, it is well for the manager to work with them separately to assure that desired changes are accomplished.

✼✼ 6 ✼✼

Holding People
Accountable for Performance

✼✼ ✼✼ ✼✼ ✼✼ ✼✼ ✼✼ ✼✼ ✼✼

Developing a basis for accountability is one of the first things
that a manager has to accomplish in establishing positive organizational direction and climate. A manager needs to be clear with
employees about their roles and responsibilities and the results
expected in order for them to know what they will be held accountable for. While holding employees accountable for performance, the manager must be accountable to them for support.
Accountability must hold not only vertically but also horizontally, among peers and team members. A chief executive officer
(CEO) recently remarked that her organization became much
more effective and her job more enjoyable when she worked on
developing horizontal accountability with her staff. Previously,
she had been the only one who held others accountable.

Accountability may be defined as a condition of being
liable, answerable, or responsible for something of value. If
what people are doing is valuable, then it is essential that you,
their manager, hold them accountable for accomplishing it. The
message becomes clear that it is important. If people are not
held accountable, the manager is sending the message that what

they are doing is not important, not worthwhile. In work relationships, if the parties to agreements do not hold each other accountable for what they agreed to do, the relationship breaks down, leaving one or both parties with decreased feelings of self-worth and an attitude of "Who cares?" or "I am not worthwhile." When people are not held accountable for performance, permissiveness, low performance, frustration, anxiety, uncertainty, fear, and apathy may result. This chapter will give the manager tools and options to use in handling accountability. It will address the concept of joint accountability and a system for managing it that includes performance review and evaluation. Accountability is closely related to organization results and role clarification, as presented in Chapters Two and Three. In fact, results will not be fully achieved or roles kept clear unless accountability is managed effectively.

Basis for Accountability

The first step in managing accountability is to establish a clear basis of responsibilities, boundaries and limits, and the expectations that managers have of their subordinates and other managers. So that all parties are productive for the organization, standards of performance must be established to cover quantitative and qualitative areas of operations, as well as attendance and such behavioral areas as cooperation, teamwork, and adaptability, with measurable, specific descriptive criteria. It is easier to set standards in quantifiable operational areas than in service areas, where the standards must measure behavior. Another area where setting standards may be difficult is that of how a manager manages. These areas will be discussed in detail later in this chapter.

A manager also needs to let subordinates know what is expected of them in addition to the productive tasks they perform, such as the types of reports they are expected to submit. Their decision-making authority and reporting responsibility should be clearly defined, distinguishing among (1) actions they may take on their own initiative, without reporting; (2) actions that must be reported to the manager after being carried out;

(3) actions that require prior approval of the manager and should be reported to the manager once carried out; and (4) actions that might affect other departments, which should be discussed with those departments first and be reported on to the manager after being carried out. Another factor in decision-making authority is the boundaries or limits that a subordinate must operate within, such as laws, budget and financial resource constraints, and safety, security, or operating rules and regulations that affect policies and procedures. When these boundaries are clear, the subordinate knows his or her freedom to make decisions.

Joint Accountability

If you have worked on the practices described in earlier chapters, people will be thinking in terms of organization results, as described in Chapter Two. When your focus is on organization results, it becomes obvious that two or more people, or two or more units, will be accountable for the same result. For instance, when the maintenance engineer is held accountable for the availability of a piece of machinery to operate at its designed rate when needed, he or she will be jointly responsible with the operator of that piece of equipment. The maintenance engineer and the operator, knowing that they will be held accountable for this outcome as defined through role clarification, are then aware of the need to cooperate to make it happen. With this commitment to a common result, they are more likely to cooperate and keep in close touch with each other not only when there is a problem but also at other times, to prevent problems.

When managers are thinking about organization results, they will see how they and their employees are contributing to the mission of the organization and will know why their jobs are important. Their consciousness is first the total organization perspective, second their unit's result, and then their individual activity. Organizational success has priority over individual and unit achievement. This leads to a willingness of the manager and subordinates to confront others when they are not carrying out their responsibility.

A three-way accountability in an organization came to our attention recently. The project was the construction of a new facility at one of the firm's plants. The outcome desired was the operation of the new facility to improve productivity by a certain time within certain cost limits. The three groups involved were the design engineers, the construction division, and the people who would operate the new facility. These three units had to work together to accomplish the agreed-upon outcome, and no one would fully accomplish it until the new facility was in full operation, achieving the improved productivity desired. There were probably some other areas of accountability in this project, such as keeping the normal operations of the plant from being disrupted and ensuring that there was cash available to meet financial commitments as the work on the project progressed. It is obvious that, to complete a project of this type successfully, a number of managers of different units and their employees had to be talking to each other often and at appropriate times, giving and asking for help, confronting each other, and ensuring that there were no surprises. There also had to be some training for the plant personnel to operate the new facility, thereby involving the training department early in the process.

Joint accountability has to be managed by the managers of the people who must cooperate to accomplish the common goal. In the case of the maintenance engineer and the machine operator jointly accountable for the machine's operating as designed, the managers of both the engineer and the operator will each evaluate their subordinates' contributions to this organization result. This may mean that the manager of the engineer talks to the operator and the manager of the operator talks to the engineer to evaluate how well they are cooperating. They should also have factual data on any downtime of the equipment and its effect on overall productivity. These managers should be held accountable by their superiors for managing their subordinates in this manner. This managerial accountability will be discussed in greater detail below.

It may be necessary at times for the manager to confront employees strongly if there are blocks to cooperation and the outcome is not satisfactory. A recent incident in a client system pointed this up dramatically. The director was aware that a potentially dangerous situation might arise if a certain problem were not remedied. It required the cooperation of two managers on the same level to work together to solve the problem, which had been brought to their attention several months previously without any results. The director called the two managers together and told them to clear up the problem within two weeks. At the end of that time, he walked through the facility and found that nothing had been done. He then called the two together and told them that if the problem was not resolved within another two weeks, both would be written up for unsatisfactory performance, and this would affect their merit rating. The problem was resolved in one week, and the two managers found that they enjoyed working together to achieve a common result. Unfortunately, when there is continued nonperformance, it is sometimes necessary for the manager to issue a threat of negative consequences. As McGregor (1960) stated in describing Theory Y assumptions, the threat of punishment is not the only way to get performance, but it *is* one way.

A System for Managing Accountability

We have found it helpful to use a model in managing organizational accountability. In this way, we are able to see how all the parts of the management process fit together. Our model (shown in Figure 1), which was developed in *Making MBO/R Work* (Beck and Hillmar, 1976, p. 117), has a navigation system for guidance and an operation system for carrying out the organization's objectives.

Navigation System. On top of the navigation triangle is the *mission* of the organization. The mission statement will identify why the organization is in business, its philosophy, and, often, its customer or client focus. For organization direction, it is equivalent to the North Star, since it provides a reference point for all activities. Each person should know how his or her job contributes directly or indirectly to this mission. While the mission statement is written in general result terms, it serves as a basis for setting more specific objectives and criteria for evaluation.

Figure 1. MBO/R Navigation and Operation System.

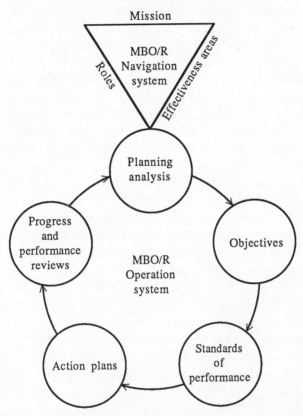

Source: Beck and Hillmar, 1976, p. 117. Used by permission.

Drucker (1954) points out that the mission is outside the organization—its focus is the customer or client. He identifies the customer as the foundation of a business, the one who keeps it in existence. The mission of the management institute of which we are members is "productive organizations and achieving individuals." With this in mind, we are aware that we are not successful until our clients are successful. Organizations get in trouble when their mission is inside their organization. It appears that this is what occurred in the American automotive industry, whose mission seemed to be producing and selling cars at a profit instead of something like "satisfying customer transportation needs." Making a profit is, of course, essential, but it must be a secondary focus, behind customer needs, or the company is destined for problems, especially in the long run.

Roles in the organization are the second side of the navigation triangle. Roles identify how the mission will be accomplished in terms of outcome descriptions and establish the functional and relationship boundaries. Roles at the management institute include consultation, education, publication, and administration. Roles for an automobile manufacturer would include research and development, production, sales, customer service, and finance. (Roles were covered in detail in Chapter Three).

Effectiveness areas make up the third part of the navigation system. These define the result areas of work that must be managed in order to be effective organizationally and individually. Organizational effectiveness areas for our institute might be public seminars, behavior change, client productivity, and publications used. For an automobile manufacturer, they might be engineering, style, safety, and comfort. The use of effectiveness areas does much to assure that a manager will manage for results rather than for activities, since the focus is on doing the right things to produce organization results.

Managers using effectiveness areas will find them helpful in identifying the outcomes they desire in their units and from their subordinates. They are particularly important in developing evaluation criteria for a management position. Reddin (1971) identified these common effectiveness areas that apply to most management positions: subordinates, innovation, projects, development, systems, and co-workers. Using these result areas, a manager and his or her subordinates can develop criteria for the condition that will exist when the supervisor is managing acceptably. For example, in the subordinate area, some criteria may be grievances, people ready for promotion, development of people, coaching, counseling, and transforming problem employees into productive employees.

The negotiation and clarification of the navigation system are an empowering process for subordinate managers. Once there is understanding and acceptance in these various areas, managers are able to put their energies into the functional management concerns from a position of agreement, knowing that their optional or discretionary managerial behavior will be evaluated against an agreed-upon base. The freedom to act with reduced stress and conflict, coupled with clear task direction, is a sure route to increased productivity in almost every case.

A forestry organization that went through the process of developing this navigation system discovered that their mission was much broader than putting out fires and managing forests—that it extended past managing fiber to recreation. Similarly, their role in the environment was expanded to include urban work as well as rural. In defining effectiveness areas, they found that some functions were being performed by more than one division and that some had been neglected and no one felt responsible for them. *Making MBO/R Work* (Beck and Hillmar, 1976) presents a more detailed description of each of the navigation system elements, as well as those of the operation system, which is described below.

Operation System. The first element in the operation system is *planning analysis.* As a connecting link to the navigation system, it ensures that the daily managing of the organization is based on the foundation established in the mission, roles, and effectiveness areas. The planning analysis includes an analysis of the internal environment, including the strengths and weaknesses of the organization and the opportunities and threats facing it. Typical internal resources assessed are labor, financial, physical, and technical resources. It also includes an appraisal of the external environment, including those factors that affect the organization's or unit's success or failure, such as economic trends, actions of competitors, technological advancements, sociopolitical changes, and so forth. A third part of planning analysis covers the organization's past performance to identify gaps and overlaps. This should be done in each of the effectiveness areas. Assumptions about the future that would have an impact on the organization make up the fourth part of the planning analysis. This includes forecasts on political, economic, scientific, cultural, social, and technological influences. These assumptions may be informed judgments or even guesses, but they will be based on known criteria and trends and predictions of authorities in particular fields.

This type of planning analysis should be done by managers and their groups at all levels in the organization. It is essential that the line organization be involved in this process. Technical planners have an important role in coordinating and facilitating, but if they do the primary planning, there is likely to be a minimal commitment by those who have to carry out the plans. The data from these four steps will provide the basis for setting priorities and objectives for both operational and strategic planning.

The next item in the operation system is *objectives*—either project objectives or improvement objectives, including self-development. We think that the number of objectives that a manager is working on at a given time should be limited to between two and five to assure that sufficient time is devoted to developing and monitoring the action plans for managing performance. Each job should be divided into areas of routine operations, emergency problem solving, and improvement. Written standards of performance will be sufficient for the routine aspects; and objectives should be delineated for the improvement aspects. We believe that a manager should spend about 20 percent of his or her time on these items. This approach can clear up some of the problems that managers have with management by objectives by not only limiting the number of objectives but also assuring that the routine aspects of the job are not ignored.

The objective-setting process between the manager and subordinate and between individuals and teams is crucial to obtaining commitment to the goals of the organization. This is an eyeball-to-eyeball negotiation process in a climate of openness. Realistically, the negotiation process does not always result in total agreement; there are some organization needs that an employee may disagree with but must accept and support. Managers have the right to demand this acceptance. However, the manager can give the employee freedom about how the goals are achieved. At times, it will be impossible to achieve certain personal objectives in the organization. This needs to be openly addressed so that individuals can decide to change their objectives, accept the fact that they cannot meet them, or change to different jobs in the organization or elsewhere, so that they can achieve their career and life aspirations.

Routine aspects of the job should be subject to written *standards of performance,* descriptions of output conditions that exist when a job is being performed acceptably. They are both quantitative and qualitative. Usually, it is not possible to describe a job completely with quantitative standards. In these cases, the manager will have to work with the employees to establish subjective criteria as standards for evaluation. *Goal Analysis* (Mager, 1972) is recommended to managers as a good reference to help in the development of standards in hard-to-measure areas. Mager's "Hey Dad Test" and goal-analysis procedure are especially helpful in developing observable results-oriented behavior in goal statements.

The process for setting standards is the same used for setting objectives. Managers should inform employees of their expectations and needs, and employees should tell management what they can do with available resources. This provides the basis for the negotiation process. Though some standards may not be negotiable, the "how" of meeting them and the resources available are usually negotiable. When standards are agreed upon, managers should see that feedback systems are set up to let the employee and the boss know when the individual is meeting standards. In addition to the negotiation process between manager and subordinate, it is necessary for some standards to be negotiated horizontally—between peers—to ensure compatibility and support. In managing standards, the manager receives the feedback needed to know the level of performance. If it is acceptable, the manager does not need to talk with the subordinates about these routine operations, but if it is unacceptable, it should be discussed. When the standards are not being met, the boss and subordinate or team need to discuss the problem and agree on a plan to remedy the situation and prevent it from happening again. There are times when it is appropriate to change a standard. This is a time when the manager should negotiate an improvement objective. When a detailed plan is developed, the manager and subordinate can pay special attention to the situation.

One manager remarked on how he worked with employees who were not performing satisfactorily. First, there had to be agreement on the standards. When standards were not being met, the manager discussed this with the subordinate or team to determine what was causing the unsatisfactory performance. Then the subordinate or team was given the task of preparing an objective and plan of action to improve performance to an acceptable level and maintain it there. This plan was then managed and the subordinate or team held accountable for carrying it out satisfactorily. Sometimes the manager was part of this improvement plan by managing differently and/or providing resources in a more supportive manner.

Action plans are essential for accomplishing objectives. It has been said that an objective without an action plan is a dream or a forecast. We find it nearly impossible to manage the achievement of an objective without a detailed action plan covering resources (personnel, material, and financial) needed, the individuals or units involved, and strategies for overcoming the barriers to accomplishment. With this plan, the feasibility of the objective will become apparent. If it is not feasible, it may be necessary to go back to the planning-analysis or objective-setting phase to determine whether it should be scrapped, altered, or delayed. The involvement of the people needed to achieve the objective will result in a higher commitment on their part and, consequently, in a higher chance of success. Such plans are an excellent basis for managing accountability.

Some of the pitfalls, or errors, in action planning are (1) devoting insufficient time to it; (2) not involving those needed to carry out the plan; (3) not carrying out steps in sufficient detail or specificity; (4) disregard for checkpoints or failure to hold people accountable for meeting dates; (5) allowing the plan to become an end in itself rather than focusing on getting the job done; (6) not recognizing that some activities can go on concurrently; (7) failure to review progress at intervals; (8) failure to evaluate overall performance; and (9) failure to be aware of the group process in goal setting and checkpoint meetings. A manager who allows these pitfalls to exist is engaged in negative practices.

Progress and performance review is the last step in the operation system. The manager closes the loop at this point, and the system then functions in a continuous recycling process that includes planning, objective setting, establishment of standards and criteria of performance, action plans, and progress and performance reviews. The payoff from constant review and evaluation is improvement in performance, prevention of unsatisfactory or mediocre performance in the future, development of people, and a clear, understandable basis for administering rewards. It also serves as a diagnostic tool to determine what to work on next to improve both individually and organizationally.

An essential element in review and evaluation is appropriate feedback systems that provide the necessary data to assess progress and performance. A manager needs to be sure that employees know how these feedback systems work, who does what and when, and how the feedback data will be used. An effective feedback system is one in which the people doing the job receive information in a form and at a time that allows them to compare performance with standards and to take corrective action if necessary. Some primary sources of information are accounting reports, sales records, visual inspection, internal surveys, external surveys, and secondary data. Observation and talking to people are effective means to find out what is going on. This is easily handled when the manager circulates among employees talking to them and being open to their comments. The buzz words for this style of managing are "management by walking around." This type of feedback system may be considered "spying" if the information is used inappropriately.

An example of effective use of this system in a nonthreatening way is a top executive who would wander through departments speaking to people, every now and then stopping to ask an employee what he or she was doing. After receiving an answer, he would ask "Why are you doing this task?" The usual answer was "I don't know" or "We have always done it this way." The boss's usual reply was "Hmm, that's interesting. Thanks." He then moved on, making a mental note. After one such occasion, he wandered by the supervisor's station and asked, "Do you know what Susie is doing over there? She said she was doing it because it had always been done that way. I think we should look into whether there is a better way of doing that job. What do you think?" When the supervisor admitted that he was not sure why they were doing it that way, the boss commented, "I would like you to explore other ways of doing that job. Let's talk it over in a couple of weeks." Later, a specific date was set. Out of this dialogue came a new system for processing paper with a team approach that cut the time considerably and gave the customer faster and better service. The employees developed teamwork, enjoyed their work more, and knew why their job was important in serving the customer. This particular manager turned a negative operation into a very positive one. Customers felt this change with better, faster service from very pleasant clerks who were committed to serving them.

We advocate that managers hold at least quarterly progress reviews, in addition to the formal performance review held annually. For new employees or for old employees with new assignments, weekly reviews may be appropriate. These reviews may be very informal, take only a few minutes, and be done at the worker's work station. One effective way for a manager to handle these reviews is to respond to "incidents" as soon as possible, giving both positive and negative feedback about the performance or behavior. In this way, the employee receives frequent feedback on his or her performance and has an opportunity to rectify unsatisfactory performance as soon as it is identified, instead of receiving feedback only at the annual review or, in some cases, never receiving it until there is a reduction in force or a restructuring that leaves the employee without a job. Confronting early on is a more human and caring way of managing accountability and can be developmental for the employee. Positive feedback given in this manner lets the employee know clearly what the manager sees as acceptable performance.

There probably has been more written on performance reviews, or performance appraisals, than on any other management subject, and yet they continue to be handled poorly. We believe that this occurs because of fear or guilt on the part of the manager, lack of ongoing dialogue during the year, inadequate feedback systems, inadequate or unclear standards and criteria for evaluation, and failure to focus on the development of people as the primary reason for performance reviews. For managers and supervisors to handle these reviews more effectively, they must have training in interpersonal skills, be supported and held accountable for doing the reviews in a developmental manner, have consulting help when needed in problem situations, and have models from the managers above them on how to conduct the review. There also needs to be training to achieve reasonable uniformity in evaluation from one manager or department to another.

Performance reviews often are considered to be only a personnel system, administered by the personnel department. They need to be recognized as a vital part of the managerial process, which includes managing accountability. When the approach we have described is followed and appropriate details negotiated and agreed upon, the systemic basis is there for managing and appraising to produce what most people working with appraisal systems seek: a process that can identify managerial behaviors to be developed for organizational effectiveness, a tool for supporting personal development needs, a basis for identifying an individual's performance and potential, and, increasingly, a total system that meets legal requirements.

Managing Support and Accountability Simultaneously

Once roles are clarified, direction established, and objectives and priorities set as a part of the overall planning process, the actual managerial effort becomes a day-to-day function. This total effort will initially require considerable work and commitment by a manager, but it will quickly begin to provide the basis for managing with a focus on organization results.

When a manager becomes aware of unsatisfactory performance, he or she should give immediate feedback and confront the performer with the facts to determine what is wrong, how it can be corrected, what help is needed, and how it can be prevented in the future. This immediate action on the part of the manager gives the very strong message that the process is "for real," that the manager is managing accountability, and that evaluation will take place. It is essential that the manager handle this feedback and confrontation in a supportive, caring way, with definite expectations for improvement and problem solving. The manager should affirm the subordinate as a person and express a belief in his· or her ability to deal with the specific situation in a more appropriate manner. The manager may then join in a problem-solving process, perhaps prescribing steps to get the job back on track and continue to develop the performance potential of the person. The manager should always ask whether he or she was a factor in the substandard performance and, if so, what could have been done differently to prevent it.

A key to managing accountability is being supportive at the same time. The two approaches work hand in hand—a both/and rather than an either/or situation. A recent experience emphasizes the value of this. A manager decided that he needed to change his style of managing because the job was not getting done. His department heads were frustrated and not talking to him. As a result of an organization-development effort, he became aware that he had been avoiding the managing part of his job, since he preferred doing things himself. Gradually, he made his department heads aware of his expectations and the fact that he was going to start holding them accountable for performance. As he had suspected, the performance of three of his six department heads was unacceptable or marginal. When the unsatisfactory performers became aware that they were going to be held accountable, both found a way to leave the organization—one retired, and the other obtained another job. The manager worked supportively with the marginal performer without success for over a year, and then this department head also retired. Two of these three were replaced by top performers who accepted managing accountability and providing support, and the duties of the third were assumed by others. The remaining department heads relished the manager's new style and improved their performance. The message in this illustration, we think, is that when the boss manages "for real," people generally shape up or find a way to get out—gracefully or, sometimes, not so gracefully.

If you, the manager, take risks and innovate, you will have some failures. When this occurs, admit it and take corrective action. Modeling this behavior conveys the message that

there will be some failures and mistakes, which will be identified and corrected. We must be open to learn from our mistakes
and failures. The manager using positive practices expects that
there will be problem solving to improve performance as soon as
there is an awareness that something is wrong. In fact, the manager should expect subordinates to come to him or her as soon
as they are aware that they are having trouble. This establishes
the norm that it is all right to ask for help—in fact, that subordinates are expected to ask for help rather than cover up and
deny that anything is wrong. This does not suggest tolerance of
repeated mistakes and failures on the same standard. When a
subordinate is unable or unwilling to correct or eliminate unsatisfactory performance, the manager has the responsibility to
discuss the issue of new duties, new job, demotion, or severance, whichever is appropriate. However, every effort should be
made to help subordinates get up to standard before disciplinary measures are implemented.

   This process of ongoing review and dialogue makes it possible for the subordinate to make corrections in performance
and for the manager to coach or counsel when needed. It provides the opportunity for both parties to keep their relationship clear and resolve any conflicts before they become major
issues and barriers to their working relationship. It also eliminates any surprise that may occur when the only feedback on
performance occurs during the annual performance appraisal,
including the devastating experience of an employee being dis-
missed for unsatisfactory performance that he or she was unaware of. These reviews are also good opportunities for the boss
to give the subordinate rewards in the form of positive recognition for a job well done. When this dialogue is open and straight,
there will be less fear, and the subordinate will have a higher
motivation to risk new ideas and confront problems or barriers
to performance.

Formal Performance Review

   The annual performance review is a continuation of the
day-to-day reviews and a closing of the loop in the managerial
process. When regular progress reviews are held, the annual per-

formance review will be much smoother and less traumatic and will probably require much less time. It is desirable for both the manager and the subordinate to prepare in advance and have notes on all aspects of the review for discussion during the actual interview. This is also a good time to discuss the subordinate's career plans and set objectives for the next year with the subordinate. Some people advocate separating performance review and salary review. If the annual performance appraisal has been "difficult" and the outcome of the discussion significantly affects the salary adjustment, it is desirable that they be separated. The basis for determining salary adjustments should be performance during the year, not this interview; eventually, however, the manager must tie the two together, because they cannot be separated in his or her mind in making a decision.

The reason that managers do not conduct effective performance reviews of subordinates is often deeply personal, involving some form of fear. Sometimes fear stems from a feeling of inadequacy. Managers who have never received or given a meaningful performance appraisal may not know how to conduct one. In an organization with no working models of performance appraisals, there is a need for training and support from both managers and peers. A manager might also have a fear of failure: fear that the subordinate will become angry and resist the manager's suggestions or even quit speaking to or liking the manager; or that the manager might be wrong and that the subordinate might challenge the evaluation. These fears might stem from a negative experience that the manager has had in the past, either with a superior or with subordinates. In any event, when a manager is locked up with fear, he or she will either avoid the performance appraisal or conduct it in an ineffective way: punitively, with anger, or permissively, with indifference.

The process described above will help to significantly reduce or eliminate the fears that many managers and supervisors have. The basis for open and genuine relationships is established through developing a shared understanding about values, organization results, roles, and effectiveness areas and through being straight with others and clear with yourself about yourself. Where some of these elements are lacking, the organization will require an ongoing training effort to build the necessary managerial skills and competencies as well as the supportive structure.

Though over a decade of study, research, writing, training, and practice has gone into seeking to improve performance reviews, the situation today is not significantly better than or different from what it has been historically. Though we know the skills, techniques, and practices that should produce a better outcome, it still is not happening. Accountability for managerial performance seems to be where the process breaks down. We believe that *all levels* of management must bring accountability into more widespread application.

After establishing the basis for accountability, which may take several months, the next step is doing it, being answerable. This means that there will be some form of confrontation when one party does not perform or behave in the agreed-upon manner. Positive practices for confrontation are discussed in the following chapter. The manager who may have some fears here will find helpful tools and techniques for personal development in Chapters Eleven, Twelve, and Thirteen.

7

Confronting Others in a Tough yet Supportive Way

In managing accountability, managers have to confront nonperformers, people who break agreements, and others who cause the organization to be less effective. This positive practice is a key to a manager's effectiveness and to obtaining commitment and motivation from those working with him or her. Managers confronting others in a caring, supportive way are more likely to solve problems, build trust, and develop both short- and long-term productive working relationships.

If confrontations are avoided or handled destructively, the manager will be less effective. If the problem is avoided, it continues and in most cases becomes larger and more difficult to handle. If the problem is handled destructively, such as by blaming, attacking a person's character, or chastising, the manager is destroying trust and damaging the working relationship. While this may achieve the behavior that the manager wants in the short run, he or she will have a poor relationship in the long run because of the lack of trust and the fear and hostility that often occur. Others may retaliate later with intentional or unintentional unsupportive behavior or even sabotage of the manager's decisions.

For some people, the word *confrontation* may conjure up many negative emotions, such as fear, anger, anxiety, and uneasiness, and invoke negative thoughts, such as "What have I done this time?", resulting from bad experiences that have occurred in the past, inside or outside of the organization. However, others may have positive feelings of joy and relief—"It's about time we sat down and ironed out our problems" or "I look forward to getting straight with the boss."

Confrontation may occur when one person does something that causes another person to reflect upon, examine, or change some aspects of behavior. It may also be experienced as something you do for yourself. It requires you to accept others' wants as legitimate and speak up directly for your own. Our general experience in working with managers has been that confrontation is usually avoided or handled poorly. When it is avoided, and problems reach a point where action has to be taken, it is often done in a brusque or noncaring manner. Such confrontation usually comes as a surprise to the other person. In organizations where the norm is to avoid confrontation, managers and employees usually complain to a third party about a problem they have with another employee. This results in poor working relationships, unsatisfactory productivity, a negative atmosphere, and considerable stress.

Instead of looking at confrontation in a negative way, we suggest that managers look at it positively. When you do not confront a person about unsatisfactory performance or behavior or broken agreements, you may be sending messages such as "I don't care about you," "I did not expect you to do it anyway," or "It wasn't important." Such messages are demeaning and show a lack of caring for the other person. When managers look at confrontation as a caring process, they are saying that they want to solve problems, want a good working relationship, and expect that others want the same. Confronting in a supportive way communicates that the manager cares about the other person as a human being by giving the other person the opportunity to change once he or she is aware of what the concern or problem is. It also communicates that the manager cares about the success of the organization and will confront any behavior that is damaging or threatening to it. Finally, confrontation shows that the manager cares about him- or herself, because avoidance of confrontation causes the stress of discomfort, anger, and fear. Not only is this stress harmful to the manager physically and psychologically; it blocks his or her open communication and overall effectiveness.

You, as manager, need to be aware of what keeps you from confronting others when there is a problem. The greatest inhibitor is the fear of what might happen during the confrontation or afterward—fear that the other person may not like you or may stop speaking; that you may not be able to handle the other person's reactions; that the confrontation may cause problems in the system; that you may discover that you are wrong and have to "eat crow"; or that you may hurt the other person in some way and that he or she may not be able to take it. Managers can imagine all sorts of negative results that may not be real. Part of the preparation process will be to check out these fears and imaginings to test their validity.

Preparing for Confrontation

To assure positive results from confrontation, an orderly preparation is helpful. The first issue is to determine whether you want to confront the other person. The following activities and questions will be helpful preliminary steps in making this decision while raising your awareness of the blocks and risks involved:

1. Think of and describe a person or situation you need to confront.
2. What are you doing about this situation? Actions/inactions?
3. What are the consequences (results) of your actions or inactions? What is happening?
4. What do you want to do about this situation?
5. What stops you (inside and outside yourself) from doing what you want to do about the situation?
6. What is the worst thing that could happen to you if you did what you want to do?

7. What is the best thing that could happen to you if you did what you want to do?
8. What course of action seems appropriate, and what do you expect to result from that action?

In working through these eight steps, you will develop your options: (1) to confront the other person, (2) to accept the behavior of the other person, or (3) to withdraw from the relationship. You can also consider the risks that fall into three categories: (1) risks you can take, (2) risks you cannot take, and (3) risks you cannot afford not to take. These are significant considerations in deciding whether to act.

Being prepared for the confrontation itself is important. Though you may not have to use all of them for each instance, the following preparation activities are suggested:

1. Get the facts and have them readily available. This includes original agreements, written data, observations, information from other persons, dates, and so on.
2. Reflect on the situation, the data you have, and your feelings and thoughts. The data from the preliminary steps listed earlier should be supportive. It is helpful to discuss the situation with a third party, a support person who will listen and challenge you without judgment and advice. Practice the interview by having your support person assume the role of the person you plan to confront and answer you as you would expect that individual to answer. After going through the interview, exchange places with your friend and repeat the interview. This step is probably necessary in very difficult situations where the manager feels immobilized with fear and anxiety. It can be quite useful to experience the situation from the other person's perspective.
3. Validate the outcome condition that you decided on in preliminary step 8. Refine or clarify it so that you are clear about what you want.
4. Be in a calm state of mind. Free yourself of anger, hostility, or desire for retribution toward the person to be con-

fronted. Diffusing anger is difficult, and each manager has to find the way that works best for him or her. Suggestions for coping with anger are presented later in this chapter.

5. Get in a positive frame of mind through affirmations and visual images. Affirmations, which are described in depth in Chapter Thirteen, are supportive statements in the present tense, such as "Things are working out well" or "I am listening and open to the other person's ideas." Repetition of these or similar statements and construction in your mind of visual images showing a satisfactory solution to the problem help you to go into the confrontation with positive thoughts and expectations.

Interview Guidelines

After completing the preparation work, follow these guidelines in carrying out the interview:

1. Negotiate a time and place to suit the other person.

2. Speak from the "I." We are experts on ourselves—we know what we are thinking, feeling, seeing, hearing, and so forth. We do not know any of this about the other person. Avoid using the word *you,* as it puts the other person on the defensive. An example of the difference is shown in the following illustration:

> An employee has promised a report to the manager by noon on Monday. It is now Tuesday afternoon, and the manager does not have the report. If the manager charges the other person with "You did not do that report that you agreed to give me by noon yesterday," and the report has been completed, an argument might ensue. Instead, the manager can avoid an argument by confronting with what she knows: "I do not have the report that you promised me yesterday. What happened?" This leaves it open for problem solving. The employee might reply, "I finished that report several days ago and sent it to you. Let's check on what

happened. It may have been delayed in the mail system, gone to the wrong office, or got mixed with other papers."

We often hear that this is all well and good, but what if it is my boss whom I need to confront? The same principles apply, with an emphasis on how you can support your boss. For example, the boss has not given you the information you need or has not been clear on what he wanted you to do. The dialogue may go as follows: "It is important that I be supportive of you and help you in any way I can. I really get frustrated when you do not give me the information you promised or you have information that I need and do not pass it on to me. I want to be straight with you and have a good working relationship, but when this happens, I get angry and stop talking, which I want to change. Is there anything that I am doing that displeases you or that you do not consider supportive? If there is, I want to do everything possible to correct the situation." The key is to stay in the positive, be calm, and verbalize the desire to support and to have a good working relationship. It is important not to get angry when the boss is angry; stay calm and let the boss do the talking until the anger has subsided. You might comment as follows: "I understand that you are upset. I would be upset too if I were in your place. I would like to do whatever I can to help you."

3. Stick to the facts. Talk about performance and behavior. Avoid blaming or criticizing the other person's character with statements such as "That was a dumb thing to do," "You know better than that," or "How could you be so stupid?" Avoid guessing about the other person's motives. Avoid questions like "Why did you do this?" Ask open-ended questions, starting with what, how, when, and where.

4. Actively listen to the other person. He or she may have data that you do not have. It is necessary for good problem solving to have the thoughts and feelings of the other person. If you find that you are not listening or that you are planning what you are going to say while the other person is talking, repeat or summarize what the other person has said to verify

that you have received the message correctly. Further, make sure that you have been heard and that your message has been received correctly. A good way to stay in contact with the other person and to enhance your listening is to maintain eye contact. When you are looking into the eyes of the other person, it is difficult not to listen.

5. Keep the desired positive outcome in mind during the interview and look for ways to be supportive of the other person to ensure that result.

6. If you become emotional during the interview, especially with fear or anger, it is helpful to talk about the feeling from the "I" position. Accept that feelings are legitimate for both you and the other party. Verbalizing your emotions is relaxing for you and leads to a closer relationship with the other person. As an alternative, you may want to take a break to calm down.

7. Get on with problem solving on how the situation can be remedied and prevented in the future. Go for a solution that both people can live with. Negotiate agreements with the other person on your working relationship and how each can be supportive of the other. If the issue seems unresolvable, experiment —try another approach. Be patient! It may take a little more time.

Being calm, keeping positive thoughts, and expecting a positive outcome will be reflected in the tone of your voice and your nonverbal behavior. The words you use are important, but if your voice tone and body language do not project the same meaning, the other person receives conflicting messages. An example of this incongruency was the executive who was confronted by a colleague: "I think you are angry." He replied in a loud voice, while hitting the table with his fist: "I am *not* angry." The following are some techniques for handling anger and hostility within yourself:

1. Accept the fact that anger is a legitimate feeling and normal for human beings. Also, be aware that you are angry because you are not getting something you want. Until you are clear about what you want, you will continue to repeat the same process.

2. Take responsibility for your own anger. You made yourself angry, as you had a choice whether to be angry. No one can make you angry! To help yourself take this responsibility, repeat to yourself: "I choose to be angry."

3. After taking responsibility for your anger, be careful not to take your anger out on someone else or to confront when angry. You have no right to be destructive of another person, a real possibility when you are in a state of anger.

4. Find ways that best suit you to diffuse your anger. Some suggested ways are:

   a. Talk about it to another person who will listen without judgments and provide a "safe place" for you.

   b. Write it down until it is gone. This may take twenty to thirty minutes of writing. Writing a "poison pen" letter may help; however, burn it when finished.

   c. Take physical exercise.

   d. Remove yourself from the environment—walk around the block, go home, and so on.

   e. Meditate—slow down, be silent, relax.

   f. Get close to nature—walk in the woods, go fishing.

   g. Laugh at yourself. This can be very relaxing.

   h. Go ahead and be angry as long as you are not destructive to others; for example, beat on a drum, kick a ball, chop wood, beat on a pillow, pound on the ground.

   i. Accept the fact that good people sometimes behave in bad ways. Forgiveness is often necessary to free ourselves of anger and the desire to "get back" or "punish" the other person in order to be open to problem solving and a positive outcome. When you are after retribution, you are going to lose and destroy the relationship. When you are not forgiving, be aware of who is suffering. You are probably feeling bad, both physically and mentally, are upset or uncomfortable in the presence of the other person, and are putting yourself under the control of the other person. Forgiveness not only is a freeing experience but is also healthy. Many of the inmates in concentration camps in World War II who survived the starvation diets, disease-ridden barracks, and torture were those who forgave their tormentors. As one inmate at Wuppertal remarked after seeing the Nazis murder his wife, three daughters, and two sons, "Hatred had just killed the six most important people in my life. I decided then that I would love every person I came in contact with." Forgiveness and love kept this man alive and healthy in the face of every privation.

The manager may prepare well and confront in a caring way and still meet resistance from the other person. If there is resistance, remain calm and ask exploratory questions, such as "What do you think is wrong?", "Is there something you want from me that you are not getting?", or "What would you like me to do about this?" These are open-ended questions to probe the resistance and find out why the other person is resisting. You might just state: "I think that you are resisting doing this. Would you like to talk about it?" If the other person continues to resist and refuses to change, you will have to be directive and say: "I understand that you are resisting; I do expect you to change your performance. I will be checking and talking with you about this. I am available to help you and expect you to change and ask for help if needed." If substandard performance continues, you may have to confront the person as follows: "I have done all that I can think of, and your performance is still unsatisfactory. I do not know what else to do. What do you really want to do? What type of work would you like?" This can lead to discussions on different types of work, a different job in the organization, or severance and a different job in another organization. There are limits to how long unsatisfactory performance can be tolerated.

One manager who confronted a subordinate in this manner found that the person wanted something entirely different from what was possible on his present job. As a result, the manager assisted the subordinate in leaving the job and supported him in getting a job doing what he wanted to do and was capable of doing. Once the subordinate got into the new situation, he was very successful and was rewarded accordingly by his new employer. Several years later, he thanked the manager for firing him and helping him move into a new career. This was a difficult task for the manager at the time, since the subordinate was angry with him for forcing the issue, but he had the satisfaction of knowing that what he did was best for both the individual and the organization. This was a positive practice in action.

The confrontation may result in an emotional response. Sometimes the person may cry. Offer a tissue and maybe a comment: "I can see you are upset. Would you like a few moments to pull yourself together?" or "Would you like to talk about this at another time?" If so, set another time within the next couple of days.

Anger is another response that can be upsetting. It is essential that you do not take in the anger from the other person. If you do, you will either express it and escalate the situation into an argument or suppress it, consciously or unconsciously. Suppression may lead to dumping it out at a later time on the other person, dumping it on someone else, at home or in the organization, or holding it within yourself and causing physical or emotional problems of your own. Some suggestions for handling anger in others are presented below:

1. Avoid taking the anger in:
    a. Repeat to yourself: "I am not the target." (Anger is quite often misdirected.)
    b. Use visual imagery: Visualize putting the anger in a paper bag and later putting it in a trash basket. Visualize the anger in the form of arrows that are going past you. Visualize yourself as a duck and the anger rolling off your back like water.
2. Talk about it with the person who is angry:
    a. "I sense that you are upset. Is there something I can do to help you?"
    b. "I understand that you are upset now. I would like to talk to you about this at another time."
    c. "I can see that you are upset. Was there something I did to cause you to be upset? If there was, I would like to stop doing this in the future, if possible."
3. Avoid the other person when angry or hostile, if possible.

4. Use some of the techniques listed earlier for handling anger within yourself. Keep calm until the anger is diffused, so that you can get on with problem solving on what you may be able to do in the future to help the other person. Avoid being defensive. Silence may be appropriate, or use supportive statements such as "What would you like for me to do?" If you model calmness, the chances are that the other person will gradually come down to your state and be more open to problem solving. Your voice tone and concern for the other person must communicate the same meaning as your words.

Clarity on the Basis for Confrontation

Often the outcome of a confrontation is clarity on what the manager wants from the other person. Clarity of expectations is emphasized in Chapters Three and Six. These expectations have to be very specific and understood by both persons. Several discussions are usually needed to obtain this clarity. Each party must know specifically what is expected of him or her and what will happen if those expectations are not met. Until this clarity is achieved, problems are likely.

Managers need to be aware that expectations will change and that, when they do, roles will have to be redefined and standards of performance revised to reflect the changes. Managers have the right to change jobs when necessary, but they have the responsibility to let subordinates know what the changes are and to give support and training on the knowledge and skills necessary for the new or revised job. Subordinates must also be given a reasonable amount of time to acquire new skills or knowledge.

One question we often hear from a frustrated manager is "How do I handle the nonperformer whose unsatisfactory performance has been tolerated for years and who has been given regular raises and satisfactory evaluations?" Managers have the right and the responsibility to work out performance standards with such a person and to expect those standards to be met within a reasonable time. In these cases, the manager must give all the support and training possible and be patient. It may take up to two years to rehabilitate such people or determine whether they will ever be satisfactory. If they have long tenure, it is difficult to terminate their employment. You may be able to put them into another position, push early retirement, or possibly demote them. Under no circumstances should you reward this unsatisfactory performance with monetary raises of any kind. You must be willing to "go to the mat" with unsatisfactory subordinates who refuse to improve. You may lose some appeals, but if you have been clear and honest with the subordinate and built the case, you have less chance of being overruled. Managers are entitled to satisfactory performance from their employees, and it is all right to demand this. This is working accountability and support at the same time. It is combining humanism and productivity.

Results of Caring Confrontation

In confronting in a caring way, the manager is valuing the importance of long-range positive working relationships, the self-esteem of the other person, and productivity for the organization. Caring confrontation keeps the organization's channels of communication open for problem solving, improvement in performance and productivity, and employee development. Our experience is that when confrontations are carried out in a positive, caring way, the results are nearly always positive, with performance improving and both parties feeling better about themselves and the organization. It is possible to achieve short-range improvement with a destructive confrontation (blaming, chewing out, or chastising), but the long-range effects are usually costly to both the individual and the organization. This type of confrontation generates fear and hostility and usually changes little in the short range, and these negative emotions are likely to block honest and straight communication between the people involved. Negative outcomes also result from the avoidance of confrontations. This is permissiveness and lack of caring. A subordinate may have a fear of the unknown or may assume that performance is satisfactory and consequently have no motivation to change.

Supportive confrontation is not only good for productivity; it is also good for individuals by reducing pent-up anger and hostility, reducing fear and tension, improving working relationships, making for a more enjoyable, relaxed atmosphere, and increasing commitment to the organization's goals. You, the manager, may need to work on overcoming any fears or hostility you may have if you have difficulty engaging in confrontation. It may also be necessary to work on interpersonal skills in communicating with others. If negative norms cause barriers to confrontation, objectives should be set to change these to norms that are supportive. It is also essential that managers model supportive confrontation. When people are confronting and receiving confrontation effectively, they must be rewarded for the positive behavior.

While we have used the word *confrontation* extensively in this chapter, we suggest you not use the word with the person confronted, as it may act as a "red flag." Just say: "I would like to talk with you about something that is disturbing me." It is easier to confront when the manager sees confrontation as caring about the other person, the relationship, the organization, and him- or herself. The positive practice of confronting in a caring and supportive way is essential for accomplishing organization results, clarifying and maintaining productive work relationships, and motivating and empowering people in the organization.

⚥ 8 ⚥

Empowering People
for Achievement
and Success

How much power exists in your work group or team? How do you experience your own power? What is your perception of the difference between your own power and that of others? Is power a positive aspect of your organization's operations? Even though it might not have been discussed directly, power has been an underlying consideration in earlier chapters. Clarifying values, defining purpose or vision, and establishing roles, for example, have a tie to empowerment and having power. Power is at the center of getting things done; power is the capability to accomplish something. As a manager, have you noticed that some groups and even whole organizations seem to have more power than others? In this chapter, you will learn some different ways to think about—and use—power to positive advantage for increasing productivity in your organization.

Take a few minutes, now, to become aware of and experience your own power. Be aware of your thoughts and feelings about power in general. Close your eyes and hear yourself say the word: *Power!* What did you experience about your own power? What is your response to the power of others? You might want to make some notes about the things that you thought about. Since power is a common element that bridges the gap between individuals and organizations, you will find it useful to understand your own attitudes and beliefs in this area.

Our experience has been that few individuals seek to understand this significant process in depth. Thus, managers tend to work with a limited understanding or acceptance of both power and empowerment. We describe *empowerment* as a process, or the enabling means, by which a manager and an organization can maximize the efforts and effectiveness of people in using power. *Power* is more difficult to define. The viewpoint or perspective that you start from may affect your definition. For instance, power may be viewed as forcefulness or effectiveness (Josefowitz, 1980). When examined from the forcefulness view, it will most likely be defined in terms of control and probably considered synonymous with *authority*. From the perspective of effectiveness, it is most likely to be defined as the capacity or ability to perform effectively. Which position you choose will have an impact on both your power and empowerment. We have found it more practical to avoid a single definition of *power,* since none seems to cover all situations. Instead, we prefer to use several approaches to allow greater flexibility. Our preferred definition, though, is the energy, capacity, or force to accomplish the outcome that you want. Empowerment provides the process for transforming that energy into productive work that accomplishes organization results. In the complex relationships found in today's organizations, empowerment takes on greater significance.

Think back on the information you gathered about your own notions of power. Are your impressions positive and supportive? Do they represent a position that encourages empowerment at the organizational level? Do they carry fear and anger or, perhaps, the excitement and fulfillment that are associated with getting things done? Your own prior experiences with power and your current beliefs and behaviors have a direct bearing on how you, as manager, are likely to accept and work with many of the practices that we have found to be major contributions to positive management. A positive belief system that focuses on responsibility for oneself is a primary building block.

Power and Its Use in Organizations

Since power is not a widely discussed or taught subject, most managers have a limited theory base, or map, to help them and guide them in the positive development and use of power. More often, our personal experience includes what we perceive to be the misuse of power. Your exploration of your own perceptions is likely to have provided an indication of your orientation: Is power experienced primarily as a function of authority and control over others or as a function of the ability to act in accomplishing something, one's potency or potential? From the set of beliefs and values that influence our choice toward authority or potency comes a considerable number of interrelationships that also have impact on organization structure, management style, personal relationships, organizational "goods" and "bads," flexibility, and so forth.

When seen from an authority orientation, power is perceived as finite and limited: "You don't have any unless I (the defined authority) have given it to you." This is fundamental for the traditional, hierarchical organization. It functions best when there is a high level of subordinate dependence. It builds on a perception of "power over," in which there tend to be underlying assumptions—often from previous incidents—of dominance, manipulation, victimization, and violence in some form. Certainly, those are "worst-condition" assumptions, and most situations are not that way. However, those often *are* the operating assumptions and presuppositions that guide individual behavior in many situations.

In its positive form, authority—the right to tell someone what to do and make it stick—is essential to the orderly flow of command and control in many organizational situations. In the basic structuring of an organization, there are a natural expectation (based on traditional role definitions) and acceptance of this relationship and responsibility, described as institutionalized power (Osborn, Hunt, and Jauch, 1980). French and Raven

(1959) describe five bases of power that help in understanding the acceptance of this authority-based power or influence: reward power, coercive power, legitimate power, referent power (based on identity with), and expert power. In its worst form, authority power is likely to be coercive. When it is used in its positive form, subordinates may respond without hesitation to a manager's direction that comes from several power bases: legitimate power, because the structure gives them the right to give orders; expert power, because they know more; and/or referent power, because they are such a good model to follow or use. In developing your own understanding of your subordinates, you will find it useful to know the base of your power or influence with each of them and whether that base matches your own perception of your power.

In contrast with the traditional perspective, the positive orientation is based on a notion of power and empowerment that assumes that a rich potential for performance is available in each individual. Management's challenge is to establish practices that apply potential to producing organization results. Here, the perception operates on a "power with" approach that includes assumptions of collaboration, sharing, and caring behavior. This way of working also builds on the energy, capacity, and momentum that can be created through the process: synergism, which gives you more than you might have otherwise expected. These characteristics are often described as desirable aspects associated with participative management. This notion of power has an unlimited potential for expansion and is the basis for our approach to empowerment.

In his studies on achievement motivation, McClelland (1961) identified another aspect of power that affects the management process. He described three related needs that affect psychological behavior and provide the motivation for individual action: need for achievement, need for affiliation, and need for power. The need for power was defined primarily as the need to feel strong and secondarily as the need to act powerfully (McClelland, 1975). Continuing study of these motivational areas shows that growth in handling power issues is a complex developmental process that has meaningful impact on how we relate with one another as persons while carrying out the work necessary for achievement.

Developing Your Managerial Power

We believe that it is desirable for you as a person and, particularly, as a manager to regularly work with and improve your awareness of your own power. We think of it as a commitment to living life fully and contributing fully to the organization that you are a part of. Similar to the development of organizational excellence as described by Peters and Waterman (1982), empowerment is not an instant happening; rather, it is a matter of making an infinite number of "teeny" steps, all of which are directed toward the desired outcome of individuals using their personal and organizational resources more fully. The following are some areas to develop and some possible ways to go about that exploration and development.

Self-Growth. All aspects of personal and self-development are basic to empowerment. It is important to develop for yourself an awareness of the things that are going on around you and within you. Your own personal processes have to do with what you are thinking, feeling, and doing as you function day by day. Also, it is essential that you develop your own vision or accomplishment statement that clearly sets out what you want in life, including work. The relevance of this information can be demonstrated through the structure of two sets of questions that are very useful in guiding choices or decisions. The first set is: (1) What do I want? (an outcome-oriented goal statement); (2) What am I willing to do to get what I said I wanted? (a test of commitment and assumption of responsibility); and (3) Am I getting what I said I wanted? (awareness and feedback to items 1 and 2). Item 3 feeds into this related set of questions: (4) What is happening? (awareness of what is occurring at all levels of sensual sensitivity—sight, sound, feel, smell and taste); (5) What is the meaning of that? (what theory base or "map" do I have and *use* to understand the happening in item 4 so that I can consciously choose the appropriate response to the next question?); and (6) What am I going to do about that? (the application of skills and techniques to produce a desired outcome).

Developing Models. The previous discussion also illustrates another dimension of increasing power for yourself. Models or maps to provide structural reference points are helpful for increasing the confidence with which you engage a particular course of action. The combination of "knowledge" and inner "knowing" provides power and energy to a chosen course of action.

Increasing Competency. Power is given to those who can demonstrate through performance their own abilities in terms of task or technical work, managerial skills, and personal skills. Subordinates and peers give power to those who demonstrate competency in practice.

Using Your Own Power. By using whatever power you have in a positive manner, you will enrich it and energize it while validating its potency for yourself and others.

Becoming More Aware. Constant attention to awareness is basic for growth in power. Once you know more about what is happening, you can find more situations in which you are able to develop responses that allow your power to be experienced.

Knowing What You Want and Asking for It. Our experience validates the notion that people who know what they want and go after it get more of what they want and have more operational power in their organization. Putting time and energy into getting those kinds of answers is high-payoff effort. However, people who know what they want often discover that they are perceived as different and threatening and so choose not to use much of their power.

Speaking Out. Those who are willing to speak out and identify their own position are much more likely to have power and to be thought of as powerful by others. By letting others know what you think and feel, you make it much easier for them to share more with you in a nondefensive manner. This is empowerment. The strong, silent manager is not empowering.

Confronting in a Supportive Way. Being able to confront

and still continue to be supportive is very powerful. Most people tend to see confrontation and supportiveness as mutually exclusive, though they need not be. When we become more sensitive to people's needs as individuals, there is little justification for being unable to be supportive of them while coming up against some of their differences.

The Process of Empowerment

In the process of empowerment, a manager is seeking to create a way of working together that draws out the maximum human potential from the resources available. Until they begin to think about organization results first, most managers are not very concerned about a process that gives other individuals more power. Rather, they are more likely to find themselves resolving issues of dependency in their own growth and development. As they experience more situations and develop, they resolve issues of being dependent *on* someone (others), of being counterdependent *against* others (particularly authority figures), and of being independent *from* others. When, as manager, you are able to work comfortably with these dependency issues, you are ready for the significant jump to interdependence *with*. Interdependent behavior requires a high level of sharing, which emerges as you are increasingly able to perform from your own strength and identity as a manager. Managers who have reconciled issues of their own identity are able to move more freely into sharing—empowering—relationships with individuals as well as their work groups.

It is rather difficult for a manager to engage in a participative management style without having resolved his or her own dilemmas about dependency and accountability. This is usually important for enabling managers to be comfortable with subordinates who are becoming more powerful as individuals. A major part of the delegation process is building the trust that allows for full delegation and the empowering of others to be responsible for using their potential while achieving the organization's goals.

How two people manage the handling of a canoe is a

good illustration of several principles involved in empowerment. It is helpful for the canoeists to explore how they are different in their experience and competency as well as their strengths and weaknesses on the water. If one is more experienced or has a stronger stroke, it will affect how they work together in reaching their destination. The usual role expectation is that whoever sits in the aft end will control the direction of the canoe. If this is not accepted, considerable energy is likely to be consumed in coping with subtle defiance or denial while seeking to establish one's own power. In stroking with the paddles, there has to be a balance between the two paddlers, and that interdependence has to be developed and modified while they are in the water. If the paddling is not coordinated and both end up paddling on the same side, the canoe will be going in circles in a short time.

Talbot's model (Beck and Hillmar, 1976), which is presented in Figure 2, provides a basis for understanding characteristics of power in an organizational environment. It can be used both as a "map" for knowing what to do and as a diagnostic tool in application situations. It shows a matrix relationship among the characteristics membership (M), control (C), and production (P). People concerns move from M to C to P, and work concerns normally progress from P to C to M. The initiating people issue, inclusion, interacts first with the control characteristics of norms and differences, then with the production issues of goals and communications. Similarly, the primary work or production concern, outcomes, interacts with the issues of roles and structures in the organization, then with goals and communications. Power is a central control issue that interacts with all of the other characteristics in some way. In this way of working with power, we are seeking to get the individual's energy directed toward the accomplishment that is specified as the organization outcome or result. This is a critical step for empowerment. If there is not a clear presentation of the desired result, the individual must develop it, as described in Chapter Two. Establishing organizational identity is an empowerment concern here. When individuals are provided clear direction, there is much greater likelihood that they will develop a

Figure 2. Talbot's Model of Organizational Power.

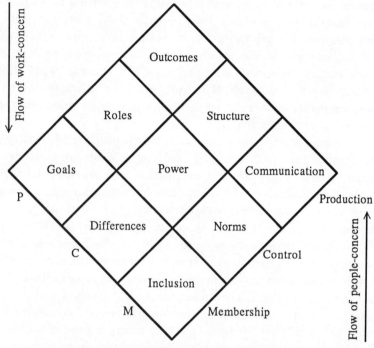

Source: Beck and Hillmar, 1976, p. 35. Used by permission.

strong identification with the organization, and membership or inclusion issues will be resolved more quickly and easily.

In the model shown in Figure 2, *outcomes* are the end results of task production that affect the organization's contribution to its environment, to its own self-maintenance, and to the people who serve in the organization. Outcomes are seen as internal and external, as tangible and qualitative, as rewards and punishments, as new potential and depletion, and as transactions and values.

Roles are symbols that identify functions and clarify relationships between members and groups within an organization. Roles represent functions and relationships that are effectively more important to the organization than to individual members. Role development is the process of identifying particular relationships among individuals or groups in performing various functions in an organization; it is clarified through human interaction, working directly with the feelings, attitudes, and behavioral relationships of the people involved.

Structure is the ordering together of people, power, and resources in bounded relationships that channel work flow toward productive goals. It is the formal identification of how the organization will do what it sets out to do and how various parts work together.

Goals are the targets toward which purposeful activity in an organization is directed. To be useful, goals are time structured, specific, feasible, and measurable and provide a basis for evaluation at some future time. They are the linking pins of purpose with the organization's environment, its internal maintenance, and the needs of the people in the organization.

Power is the energy and ability to influence decisions about people and resources. Power is taken by use and given by use but not given by abdication. Power in an organization is not used alone but is channeled through the vehicles of norms, roles, structure, and management of differences. Power is exercised personally by virtue of the way a person perceives him- or herself in relationship to other persons and groups. Power is exercised authoritatively by virtue of holding a particular position in a structure to which organizational power is assigned.

Communication is the process of sending and receiving data that have understandable meaning to both sender and receiver. Communication is used to establish human relationships, to facilitate transactions, and to transmit information needed for control and production functions. Diagnostically, the quality of interpersonal communications is a behavioral statement of the quality of the human relationship.

The management of *differences* in resources, power, or people is the key process in productive or creative effort. Work is the functional use of differences and similarities; conflict is their dysfunctional use. Differences can also be managed by avoidance. Differential management focuses internally on the development and use of people, power, and resources toward purposeful goals and externally on procurement of membership and resources and the productive and distributive return to the environment.

Norms are the unwritten rules of group behavior (the informal structure) that are initiated and maintained by collective human behavior. These are influenced initially by the expectations, attitudes, and assumptions that members bring to a group. A norm is feeling oriented and sanctioned by consensus, as the result of real or implied behavior in groups. It is operative only as long as it is reinforced by further behavior or stands unchallenged by differing behavior. Norms can be perceived as restrictive or generative, according to their influence on the effective functioning of the organizations.

Finally, *inclusion* is the process of building a relationship. It involves the feelings and behavior of people in the acceptance of similarities and differences, the building of give-receive relationships, and coping with the dynamics of acceptance and rejection.

A primary linkage exists between differences and roles. As manager, you must be working frequently with how differences are managed toward agreement rather than conflict. Differences are a natural part of the uniqueness of individuals, part of their identity. Those differences of all types have to be focused toward effective utilization. This is accomplished primarily through role-clarification activity. As described in Chapter Three, role clarification seeks to integrate individual differences into the needs of the organization and develop agreement on how individual power will be used in the accomplishment of the desired outcome. Through the process of empowerment, your organization can have a significantly higher level of energy or power available to be directed toward its achievement and success. By the way you empower individuals, you can influence the creation and flow of that energy.

When managers, subordinates, and peers achieve freedom from reliance on "shoulds" and work together in a problem-solving way, they will attain freedom for action, freedom to make things happen, to be influential, and to be powerful. Through managing differences in the role-clarification process, you transform "shoulds" into commitment responses that are based on personal involvement, identity, and agreement to be accountable for the behavior desired.

Power in Managing Individuals and Teams

Positive empowerment practices will legitimize having power or being powerful and using that power responsibly. Managers and subordinates alike often have a fear of somehow misusing their power and hurting others. That fear can be disempowering, and managers must provide a support system that encourages individuals and teams to use their power in a way that is not perceived as harmful or negative. Power is amoral—neither good nor bad of itself. Its use and the consequence of that use must be managed toward attaining a positive contribution to organization results if people are to put their full energy into being powerful. Rubin and Berlew (1984, p. 36) describe the behavior of individuals who feel powerful and believe that they can make a difference. Such individuals:

- Are more concerned with achieving results than avoiding mistakes.
- Do what needs doing rather than waiting for someone else to take action.
- Accept the risks required to achieve innovative results.
- Look for opportunities to contribute, even outside their defined area of responsibility.
- Use a wide range of contacts and resources to get the job done.
- Expect to influence peers and superiors as well as subordinates.
- Communicate directly and forcefully.

The various action items that we discuss in this book provide managers the basis for building an empowerment process. From the Talbot model presented in Figure 2, you can see that it is necessary to initially work on the inclusion or membership issue to get the individual's energy and power moving toward the organization's needs and goals. This issue has to do with an individual's sense of belonging and identity in a work group. Basic concerns here are questions such as: "Who am I in relationship to you—or the group itself?" "How good are our communications?" "Can we do something together?" and "Do we want to stay together?" Even when people have been working together for a long time and getting a job done, often neither they nor their contributions are accepted by others. Consequently, they may not have inclusion in the work group. A major concern when the team or work group is changing rapidly is "How do we make new members part of the group quickly and effectively?" A variety of the positive practices we have discussed can contribute to the inclusion effort: Values of openness and sharing might lead to some organization norms for helping new members get acquainted and accepted quickly; role clarification defines the individual's boundaries, responsibilities, and expected contributions; and the organization's vision and goals provide a clear achievement connection to significant performance accomplishments. As these various concerns are resolved, people are building their own valued "place" in the organization, leading to a higher level of acceptance and personal commitment to the organization's accomplishment.

Most of us experience some difficulty with power because it is something that is never really seen but only experienced through some other form, such as behavior. It is subjective and sometimes "scary." Many individuals we have worked with indicate a fear of (somehow) misusing power and consequently avoid accepting the power that they have or that is available to them. Building your own inner strength through values awareness provides the basis for knowing—and *accepting* —that you are not likely to apply your power in a destructive way. If you allow yourself to be disempowered by such fears, you are likely to experience hopelessness or helplessness.

Many managers find the subjective and ambiguous arena of power difficult to cope with. One way of working with these feelings in a positive, powerful way is to develop more clarity about your own power environment. You can make having power a more comfortable experience (and empower yourself) by completing the following two statements to provide information for developing understanding and acceptance: "When I am feeling powerful or am being empowered, I . . . " (list responses) and "When I am experiencing feelings of powerlessness, I . . . " (list responses). It is best to list your responses several times without looking at the previous lists and then put them together to look for patterns and specific data to build on. Typical responses have been:

Powerful	*Powerless*
have good energy	feel very dependent on others
have my goals clear	am tired and confused
speak out for my wants	avoid conflict
can say "no" comfortably	do not want any responsibility
accept differences in others	feel overwhelmed
am more trusting	am evasive
am more aware of everything	am often angry

You will want to identify your "comfort zone," where power is easily accepted, as well as behaviors that are not quite as easy. Consciously set out to find opportunities *to do more* of those positive things that are difficult for you to increase your positive comfort level. Similarly, examine the "powerless" list for patterns and situations that contribute to your sense of helplessness and then try alternative responses from your "powerful" areas. From that trial, you can develop another way of responding that will be more powerful, even if it is not as fully implemented as you might want. In this type of change, it is usually more realistic to make slower, more deliberate changes in conscious, incremental steps. It is a common tendency to go after big, highly visible pieces, which frequently become too big and are abandoned as impossible or unattainable.

As manager, you can help your own team members work through this empowerment process using these techniques. Speaking from your own experience with them adds credibility. The following examples briefly illustrate a way of working with the change process for "helplessness." A feeling of being confused may have been identified. In developing optional responses, we can ask: "What are some ways you know from your own previous positive experience to minimize or eliminate that condition?" Some possible answers might be:

- Get clear about the goal or outcome.
- Identify what is causing you confusion and what will provide clarity.
- Identify those things that you know about and those where you need help.
- Break the total effort into smaller, more manageable pieces for implementation.
- Identify who you need or what you need to get the clarity to move forward with the power of your own knowing and information.

We have found from working with managers and their subordinates while using this process that they almost always know what to do but for various reasons have disempowered themselves from using their knowledge and power in a problem-solving way. If you exercise the discipline to use your available power, it becomes much easier to keep that energy flowing. Using your know-how to get things into manageable form is basic, yet it is often passed by in times of stress.

Another positive technique for empowering individual subordinates as well as the team itself is to use structural tools that provide stability and direct the flow of activity. "Structuring is a process for shaping and channeling human energy. We create the frameworks within which interaction occurs. We create agendas, we establish job descriptions and work routines, we set up committees and task forces, we establish rules, regulations and laws, and we create institutions" (Oshry, 1976, p. 3). It is important to periodically examine whether existing structures support empowerment and energy flow or limit them. Role-clarification efforts and planning activities provide particularly useful opportunities for managers to influence structural forms of empowerment within their work groups. Positive structuring of this type provides greater freedom to manage aspects of the situation that need more personal attention. Functional structuring that provides a clear focus and supportive but not restrictive guidance will frequently eliminate or noticeably reduce resistance that may be present otherwise. Resistance tends to consume available energy in a dysfunctional way. We encourage the use of these positive techniques for managing differences toward agreement. As shown in the power model earlier, differences bridge the gap, and managing them in a problem-solving way for agreement will facilitate the flow of energy from individuals to goal accomplishment.

As manager of a working group, you can significantly improve the group's empowerment process by opening up and legitimizing the discussion of power and empowerment and making open decisions that are clearly oriented toward conscious empowerment. As a manager implementing the positive techniques we have presented in earlier chapters, you will have had a variety of opportunities to introduce power and the empowerment process:

- *Values clarification* provides many topics that are inherently part of an organization's and a manager's commitment to an environment that supports and encourages individual power through managerial action.
- The *vision* and *goal-setting* process can set structure that is empowering. Your scenario statements can clearly establish expected behaviors or outcome conditions that set the demands for a range of power applications; for example, descriptions of team members functioning as powerful individuals through the use of both their personal power and positional power. Further descriptions might set expectations for leadership and for recognition of appropriate performance.
- If it has not been started previously, initiating such action can be accomplished as part of a *role-clarification* process while discussing participation ("How can we work together in a way that will give each person fuller recognition and use of their personal potential?") or management-style expectations ("As your manager, what can I do to support your power more fully?"). It can also be done in a less formal manner during a staff meeting discussion of the topic of improving relationships and productivity.

- Positive practices concerning *norms, energy, accountability, creativity, innovation,* and others continue to provide situations in which manager, subordinates, and peers can work together in a way that provides more power and energy for the total organization.
- *Team-building* activities can be used to provide ongoing development opportunities. For example, you can develop lists of things that team members experience as empowering and those experienced as disempowering. As described above, you want to enhance and increase the application of the empowering items first. Then you examine the conditions and behaviors leading to disempowerment and develop the commitment to work with alternative responses. In such a team-building session, for example, you might want to focus discussion on enhancing the aspects of open communications that lead to more empowerment. Then, after identifying the disempowering aspects of closed communications that are experienced by the team, they can develop different ways to accomplish what is needed. If a closed situation limits information and the range of powerful responses, the team can discuss the cause of the limitation, what can be done to increase openness, and how they can acquire the needed information in alternative ways or creatively design alternative approaches to achieve greater openness. It is important that the team-building process be kept open to exploration of various issues, for this process in itself is another channel for empowerment of the group.

Organizational performance and productivity are major issues in our operating environment. While systems and technology are important and of concern, the real potential for the future lies with the managerial and personal power to energize the organization. The power model graphically shows its centrality. Our discussions and illustrations of empowerment have demonstrated the broad spectrum through which that managerial process functions. Managers who are able to empower their people and focus their energy into productive organizational effort are unique, for they come to be known as the "leaders" who can take people—the organization—far beyond normal expectations. A certain "magic" is often attributed to them. We have described elsewhere (see Chapter Four) how a team can be raised to exceptional levels of performance when its energies are brought into alignment and directed toward a productive outcome that people—the team—are committed to and an accomplishment in which they have a personal investment. In that kind of an environment, the release of creativity and innovation is highly valued and desired and is an expected part of fully using power.

𝕩𝕩 9 𝕩𝕩

Releasing
Creativity
and Innovation

𝕩𝕩 𝕩𝕩 𝕩𝕩 𝕩𝕩 𝕩𝕩 𝕩𝕩 𝕩𝕩 𝕩𝕩

How does a manager fully utilize the creativity in an organization—probably one of its most underutilized assets? Clarifying role relationships, thinking organization results, establishing supportive norms, confronting on accountability, and empowering people are some of the ways to create a positive environment where people are not only encouraged but expected to use their creative skills. Positive practices will stimulate creativity and help people to feel free to risk using these skills. The purpose of this chapter is to make managers aware of the availability of their own and others' creative skills and the choices they have in managing to fully utilize these resources. Tools and techniques will be presented for the manager to use personally as well as with others.

Innovation is essential for organizations to survive. Organizations that have been unwilling to innovate, clinging to the past, have experienced difficulties and in many cases have died. Creativity is necessary to establish and maintain a positive environment that, in turn, supports and fosters the use of creative skills in the organization. It is essential that managers cultivate creativity, as the changing environment causes a problem escalation each year; unless they unleash the creative powers in their people, their organizations will not be competitive nationally or internationally. Drucker (1974) stressed the need for creativity and innovation in his book *Management.* He stated that the organization should have a strategy for innovation and that every unit should be held responsible for it. Innovation is necessary not only in products and services but also in the social and managerial areas.

Creativity is beneficial to both the organization and the individual. Dollar payoff from implementing employees' suggestions can be high, as in the case of a young engineer in an aircraft factory. Production had been generating a sizable amount of scrap when cutting sheets of aluminum to appropriate size. The engineer suggested buying larger sheets of aluminum that could be cut into two usable pieces of equal size, with no scrap. The savings to the company exceeded one million dollars per year.

Raudsepp and Hough (1977) state that creativity is vital to an individual's psychological health. The two are interrelated. Both are associated with commitment, self-fulfillment, goal direction, enthusiasm, high motivation, and positive action. Other benefits of creativity are greater sensitivity to problems and opportunities, willingness to look at and discard old programs and attitudes as well as to break routines and rigidity in thinking, and increased capacity to look for new ideas and alternative solutions to problems. When workers have these attitudes, productivity will be high. People will feel good about themselves, their colleagues, and their organization. They will have hope and confidence in their ability to solve problems.

What Is Creativity?

Most of us were born with rich and vigorous imaginations but, sometime in our early life, shut them off. Surveys find that six-year-olds are using 90 percent of their creative skills, whereas thirty-five-year-olds are using only 2 percent ("Creativity," 1978). We are born creative, but from the first grade on, we are compelled to conform to a system that progressively constricts our freedom to imagine and create new ideas (Raudsepp and Hough, 1977). There is also the widespread mistaken notion that creativity is limited to a select few talented people in our society. Our creative powers are never lost, even though they may be submerged under many layers of nonproductive habits and blocks (Raudsepp and Hough, 1977). Consequently, the real issue is not whether people are creative but whether managers are *willing* to use what they and their employees already have.

May defines creativity as "the process of bringing something new into being" (May, 1975, p. 37). He further states that, when this breakthrough occurs, something is destroyed. When there is a creative breakthrough in art or science, the new idea will destroy something that people believe is essential to the survival of their intellectual and spiritual world. Consequently, creativity may be resisted because of the fear or guilt of destroying the status quo. This can account for resistance to encouraging creativity (May, 1975).

Other descriptions of creativity are being able to look at one thing and see another; taking seemingly irrelevant and unrelated thoughts and making significant connections that result in new patterns; and the combination of previously unrelated structures in such a way that you get more out of the emergent whole than you have put in. In other words, it is opening up to all the possibilities and discovering and accepting that there is more than one answer. This is accompanied by the self-confidence that we will solve the problem and leads to high self-worth and hope.

Barriers to Creativity

The barriers to creativity may be psychological blocks within people or external factors in the culture, in organizations, or in the methods of problem solving. We believe that creativity starts with managers themselves. Once managers are aware of these barriers, they can take steps to remove them within themselves and be supportive of those around them in

removing their blocks. They must be aware that they can remove only barriers within themselves, but they can be helpful
and supportive of others in removing their barriers.

Internal Barriers. Those barriers within ourselves are the
most difficult to remove, as they are often deep-seated and have
been a part of us since childhood. An example is a person who
learned in early childhood not to say what she thought, because
it would get her in trouble at home and in the classroom, and
so made a decision to say only what she thought other people
wanted to hear. Others may have made a decision not to disagree so as to avoid trouble. Anyone living with those decisions
will block creative ideas and not share them with others.

Internal psychological blocks stem largely from low self-
worth, which will show up in lack of self-confidence, fear, a
negative attitude, and passivity and unwillingness to change.
The lack of self-confidence is reflected in attitudes of avoidance, uselessness, and inability. It is a discounting of creative
abilities. Those who lack self-confidence may be comparing
themselves with others and concluding that they are inferior
or may be dependent on others for creative ideas and solving
problems. A manager can begin to change this negative thinking
in other people with positive feedback when they do come up
with creative ideas. The most positive feedback is using a person's idea so that he or she gets the satisfaction of seeing it
work successfully for the organization. Managers can build this
self-confidence in their employees by using their ideas even
when they may not be as good as the manager's. When an employee or group has an assignment to implement an idea of their
own, their commitment to make it work is high. If the idea
comes from management, they usually have a lower level of
commitment; if they are angry with management, they may
sabotage the idea, intentionally or unintentionally. "It wasn't
my idea," "I could have told them it wouldn't work," and
"They do not understand our situation" are comments often
heard. A manager can help overcome some of these barriers
within subordinates not only by support but also by holding
them accountable through performance evaluation for innovation and creativity. Other ideas for turning this type of negative
thinking around are discussed in Chapter Four.

The strongest block to creativity is fear. The fear may be of criticism by others, rejection, isolation, or embarrassment. A manager can help overcome this barrier by using the suggestions in the preceding paragraph and also by not being critical of others' ideas or allowing others to be critical. Always looking at the good points in an idea as well as the bad points will help overcome these fears. Always thank people for their ideas, whether you like them or not; this conveys that they are good and creative and that their ideas are wanted and valued, even though you may not use all of them.

Another internal block is a negative attitude not only about self but also about others (superiority or contempt), about the way problems are solved, and about organizations. This negative conditioning may have occurred early in our life. Anger is, in most instances, a negative emotion that will cause a block when there is a desire for retribution toward another. The fourth area of blockage is passivity and unwillingness to do anything different—being content with the way things are. This is hopelessness. A manager may overcome this block in him- or herself through human relations training, using such concepts as transactional analysis. This type of training is especially beneficial when a manager and subordinates take it together.

Environmental Blocks. Many of the environmental blocks center around resistance to change. Managers may fear change because they are unable to handle the ambiguity that goes with it or because they are guilty of smugness: "We are the best, and we have no need for improvement." This thinking can be turned around by developing the attitude that "There is nothing that we are now doing that can't be improved." Fears can be lessened when managers are confident that they and the people around them can solve any problem they have.

Another environmental block is competition and protection of territory instead of cooperation. When a manager is thinking results for the organization, he or she will find that it is essential that people cooperate and will hold employees accountable for cooperation and teamwork. This will also be his or her attitude in working with other units in the organization. Further blockage may come when there is too much to do and little time for creative thinking. Being busy is often seen as an index of productivity. When visitors from the central office come, everyone has to be busy, and all machines have to be running at full speed. The supervisor says, "I do not want anyone sitting at their desks looking out the window. I don't want any thinking around here today." One operator said, after the visit of top management, "I knew that the product I was turning out was unsatisfactory, but I did not dare stop my machine and make the adjustment that I knew was needed." When this message is given by managers, people feel that suggestions for improvement are not wanted. Managers will have to be able to explain to the visiting dignitaries that operators are responsible for quality and that this sometimes means that they must stop their machines. If the manager has difficulty explaining this to management, he or she may discuss this with the machine operators, and explaining that "busyness" is necessary on that particular day to keep management off his or her back and that their cooperation will be appreciated but that this will not be the norm of operation.

Rational scientific thinking can also be a barrier when everything has to be explained. Sometimes a person's intuition gives him a solution that he is unable to explain. Einstein dreamed his theory of relativity and spent the next couple of years working it out scientifically. Managers need to be aware of their intuition ("gut" feelings) and listen to it. Do not ignore or put down others who share their intuitive feelings. If something does not "feel" right, check it out before going further, whether you can explain it or not. A manager has the responsibility to establish a positive environment that is supportive of innovation and the creativity that comes from our intuition.

Problem-Solving Barriers. How managers handle problem solving will influence the creativity that they get from their employees and from themselves. Some of the barriers to creative thinking in problem solving are premature judgments, fast decisions, thinking only of solutions, grabbing at the first solution, or thinking that there is only one solution. A manager can reduce or eliminate these barriers by following a step-by-step problem-solving approach that will structure the process. This will assure that the problem is clearly identified and stated, pertinent information is gathered and organized in usable form, solutions and options are proposed, decisions are made on proposed solutions after adequate discussion, actions are taken on those decisions, responsibilities are defined, and evaluation times are set. A process that is flexible enough to be adapted to various situations is presented here:

1. *Define the problem.* In this step, you get clarity and understanding as to the nature of the problem. It is important here to define and verify all aspects of the problem.

2. *Gather information.* This step is concerned with collecting detailed information that documents and describes the situation, including issues and concerns.

3. *Carry out diagnosis and cause analysis.* Here you get clarity about what you want to happen as well as the meaning of what is happening. Analytical techniques such as force-field analysis can be used to focus on where the change process might start.

4. *Identify possible solutions.* Use creative ideas, "brainstorming" (see below), nominal group technique, and similar forms of idea generation to make a list of as many alternative solutions as possible.

5. *Discuss proposed solutions.* Members of the problem-solving group should evaluate the merits of each solution and rank them from best to poorest.

6. *Choose a solution.* Identify a solution (or interrelated solutions) that will produce what you want to happen. The chosen solution must be something that you can actually do as well as something that contributes to success and achievement.

7. *Do action planning.* Lay out the detailed steps for implementing the solution and identify specific steps that individuals will take.

8. *Evaluate your process.* Periodically evaluate the problem-solving process while carrying it out. Build trust and openness by discussing how you are working together and agree on ways to improve working relationships. This will be similar to role-clarification discussions.

Step 8 in the problem-solving model is the step most often over-looked by managers. The discipline of sharing observations about how the group is working together should be done regularly. If there is a barrier or a difficulty here, the manager should secure the necessary training for the group to assure that they are open with each other and willing to risk sharing their creative ideas. Allocating time to this step will assure continued improvement in the working relationships and removal of any problem-solving blocks that may exist.

A manager needs to be aware that breakdowns in problem solving usually occur in the communications process. How people talk to each other and behave with each other is critical. When there is a lack of openness and a low trust level in a group, a manager should work at opening up their communications, possibly using an outside consultant if necessary.

In this problem-solving process, it is necessary for the manager to be sure that the group is looking at the result or outcome for the whole organization, not just for their unit. What one department does always affects other departments. When a manager is aware of this, he or she can identify other units that will be affected by the decision and the help and co-operation that will be needed from other units. The manager can then invite representatives of these units into the problem-solving process at the appropriate time.

The creativity of a group is most visible in the solutions-proposing, or alternative-developing, step in the problem-solving model. Brainstorming, the Crawford slip-writing method, and nominal group technique are methods that can be used productively in this application. These techniques can be fun and energizing for getting the creative juices to flow. The following are basic ground rules for helping a group to work with brainstorming:

- *Everybody participates.* Ask each person to share at least one idea with the group before opening the floor to free flow from all. Continue to encourage participation by all.
- *Do not worry about duplication.* Getting the same idea twice is far better than not getting an idea because "it is similar"

to another. Draw out the different perspectives on the same theme.

- *Do not explain it (now).* Be brief. Put the ideas into three- to five-word phrases or, at the most, a short sentence.
- *No selling.* Just present the idea in simple terms. There will be a time later in the problem-solving process to "sell" the merits of your idea(s).
- *No evaluation.* Get the ideas out without "critical" comment. Even silly ideas, though useless in themselves, frequently provide the creative stimulation for a useful variation or new idea from yourself or others in the group.
- *Move on.* When the "flow" stops, cut off further idea generation and move to explaining, selling, and evaluating your list as responses to the problem situation.

A manager should be sure that the group disciplines itself to follow the rules so that the creative thinking process is not slowed down or stopped. When the national sales group of a company was brainstorming on how they could improve sales, one idea was "buy every salesperson a Cadillac." The boss immediately responded with the judgmental statement "We can't afford that." The group clamored, "No judgments—we are brainstorming," and the ideas continued to flow. Out of that suggestion came their decision to give a Cadillac to the salesperson of the year. It is necessary to record every idea, no matter how wild or impractical it is. Following are some questions that can be used to stimulate ideas. Ask these questions in reference to the problem, product, or service:

1. Can it be put to other uses? New ways to use as is? Other uses if modified?
2. Adapt? What else is like this? What other ideas does this suggest?
3. Modify? Change meaning, color, motion, sound, odor, taste, form, shape?
4. What to add? Greater frequency? Stronger? Larger? Plus ingredient? Multiply?
5. What to subtract? Eliminate? Smaller? Lighter? Slower? Split up? Less frequent?

6. Substitute? Who else instead? What else instead? Other place? Other time?
7. Rearrange? Other layout? Other sequence? Change pace?
8. Reverse? Opposites? Turn it backwards? Turn it upside down? Turn it inside out?
9. Combine? How about a blend, an assortment? Combine purposes? Combine ideas?

The Crawford slip-writing method can be used to collect ideas from a group in a few minutes. It will preserve some anonymity when members of the group may not be comfortable sharing their ideas in an open, verbal process. The steps are as follows:

1. Each person is given about twenty-five slips of notepaper or 3 x 5 note cards.
2. The leader presents a problem, such as "How can we improve our service to customers?" In most cases, the problem statement will have been presented in advance so that members of the group have time to reflect on the situation and incubate ideas.
3. The leader explains the importance of withholding judgments on all ideas.
4. Each idea is written on a separate slip of paper.
5. Using boxes at convenient spots, the slips are collected. The continuing process is described to participants, and a time is set for reconvening. A subgroup then sorts the slips into categories of related ideas, such as usefulness, impact, originality, and cost.
6. At the next meeting, the categorical sort is presented to participants for further discussion in small groups and a general session.
7. Additional meetings are scheduled, as appropriate, for further discussion, refinement, and selection of a course of action for the ideas that are accepted for implementation.

The nominal group technique (Delbecq, Van de Ven, and Gustafson, 1975) brings people together in a structured, nonverbal process that allows little interaction initially. Since "groups" are normally expected to be highly verbal and interactive, this restriction makes it only a "nominal" group. Thoughts are presented through a controlling procedure that leads to a group judgment reflecting the mathematically derived ranking and sorting of the important concerns shared by the group members. However, once the basic thoughts are introduced, the process provides group members the opportunity for full, verbal exploration of ideas and creative responses to problems and the decisions that must be made. Good results can be obtained by following the step-by-step process presented below:

1. A clearly defined problem statement is prepared to identify exactly what the issue or concern is. It is sent out in advance and discussed at the opening of the meeting for clarity and understanding of the problem.
2. A recorder is appointed. Notes are kept on a chart pad or blackboard where all can see them.
3. Everyone is asked to write a short personal response to the problem statement. This may take the form of a list of several optional solutions or a list of various concerns, depending on how the original statement was phrased.
4. Each individual reads his or her "first" response, and the responses are recorded on the pad. Only questions for clarification or understanding are accepted at this point; there is no discussion or evaluation. Repeat until all responses are recorded.
5. Open discussion of each item now takes place. Clarity, meaning, and expansion of ideas are important here, though a close control of time and focus of the discussion needs to be maintained.
6. What is done next depends on the preceding discussion. The leader may call for a ranking of the top five priority items as presented or ask each person to list his or her view of the major categories of action.
7. Each person's *first* choice is recorded, using the process described in step 4.
8. These first choices are discussed, using the process as above.

9. Decisions about the course of action on these "significant" items are made on the basis of the discussion and ideas presented.

Characteristics of a Creative Manager

Creative managers are distinguished by the fact that they can live with anxiety even though a high price may be paid in terms of insecurity, sensitivity, and exposure. They are also characterized by flexibility, sensitivity to problems, originality, openness to feelings and the unconscious, persistence and concentration, ability to think in images, ability to toy with ideas, ability to analyze and synthesize, tolerance for ambiguity, and anticipation of productive periods. These characteristics apply not only to creative managers but also to any creative individual. Recognizing them, a manager is able to identify those individuals in the organization who are creative.

To develop the creativity in a group, a manager has to be willing to absorb risks taken by subordinates, comfortable with half-developed ideas, willing to "stretch" company policy, able to make quick decisions, a good listener, and free to let go of and not dwell on mistakes and must enjoy his or her job. All of this can be generalized by saying that the manager has high self-worth and a high regard for other individuals. With this come positive feelings and emotions and an ability to concentrate without being blocked, as well as an inner quietude that enables creative ideas to come into his or her consciousness. The creative manager is aware of the balance that is needed and makes deliberate efforts to achieve it in him- or herself and in others. Positive and negative energies are operative and being utilized, as are the logical and the creative. The total human resource is being used productively.

Training for Creativity

The positive practices presented in this book all support using people's creative skills for productivity. Managers set the stage for creativity and innovation by demonstrating that they are valued organizationally. They also provide direction with a positive vision and goals, letting people know why creativity is necessary in their role. When using positive practices, managers will be generating positive energy and establishing norms that are supportive of a positive environment and creativity and innovation.

While creativity can be a part of management development, we recommend special training for teams and problem-solving groups to stimulate their creative skills. This training can include exercises to expand the mind and get people using the creative parts of their brain. Some of the books that have exercises of this type are *Brain Power* (Albrecht, 1980); *The Possible Human* (Houston, 1982); *Mind Games* (Masters and Houston, 1972); *The Magic of Your Mind* (Parnes, 1981); *How Creative Are You?* (Raudsepp, 1982); and *Creative Growth Games* (Raudsepp and Hough, 1977).

Workshops on developing creative skills, mind control, and mind expansion will help managers and their teams or project groups to discover and gain confidence in their creative skills. Some of the organizations conducting these workshops are: Creative Education Foundation, Buffalo, N.Y. 14213; Applied Creative Services, Laurel Drive, Lake Lure, N.C. 28746; and Center for Creative Leadership, P.O. Box P-1, Greensboro, N.C. This type of training is productive at all levels in the organization, as shown through work-simplification and quality-circle training, which include creativity as part of the program. One industrial study showed that after creative problem-solving training, the number of creative suggestions and the dollar awards doubled. There was not only an increase in the ability or willingness to make suggestions, but also a greater acceptance of them.

Another way that a manager can stimulate creativity is to reward those who share their ideas. The rewards may be extrinsic or intrinsic. Extrinsic rewards come in the form of positive strokes, special recognition or assignments, promotions, and money. On most jobs, there should be a category in the performance reviews for creativity and innovation, so that not only are people rewarded for creativity, it is expected of them, and they are held accountable for it. Intrinsic rewards are within an individual—the satisfaction of seeing a creative idea accepted, used, and implemented successfully.

The use of support groups, as explained in Chapter Eight, is another way that a manager can encourage the development of creative skills. Working with others who have the same goal gives the support and encouragement that people need. The commitment, renewal, and sharing are helpful in developing self-confidence and reinforcing the new behavior desired. Other tools and techniques that a manager can use to release creative skills are discussed in Chapters Eleven, Twelve, and Thirteen. These include managing stress holistically so that people are able to prevent and effectively cope with depression, negativity, and problems to keep well physically, mentally, and spiritually. In Chapter Thirteen, affirmations, visualization, and imagery are described in detail. Managers can use these techniques themselves and encourage those around them to do the same. We recommend offering this type of training on a voluntary basis to people in your organization.

ꙮ 10 ꙮ

Developing
Teamwork and
Interdependent Thinking

ꙮ   ꙮ   ꙮ   ꙮ   ꙮ   ꙮ   ꙮ   ꙮ

"No one cooperates here." "Our problem is communication."
We have heard comments like these from managers talking
about their organizations. One purpose of positive practices is
to remedy situations where people in organizations are not cooperating or talking straight to each other. When managers
understand the principle of interdependence, they know the
need for establishing collaborative relationships in their organization. When people are working interdependently, they use
their power and energies together to solve problems and increase their effectiveness. They confront and hold each other
accountable, empowering each other and using their creative
skills freely. The purpose of this chapter is to help managers
understand the importance of interdependence and how they
can use positive practices to develop and maintain it. It is a
necessary building block to establishing teamwork at all levels
in the organization.

Interdependence is seen as essential when managers focus
on organization results. When a department such as production
or sales considers its function as finished when it produces or

sells the product, it is operating independently and may not be fully committed to satisfying customer needs. This can lead to real problems for customer service, which has the function of serving the customer after the customer has received and is using the product. When sales, production, and customer service are committed to the result of customer satisfaction, they will realize that they need each other and that no one is finished until the product is being used satisfactorily by the customer. To achieve this end, they will have to talk to each other regularly, problem solve together, keep in close contact with the customer, and give feedback to each other. This interdependent relationship will also have to exist with other departments, such as research and development, engineering, accounting, shipping, purchasing, and warehousing.

Our organizations have become so complex today that it is critical that managers develop interdependence within their own units and with other units. It will also probably be necessary to change norms and values that are in conflict. There is less difficulty when organizations are small and people are in close contact with each other and their customers.

What Is Interdependence?

Interdependence is a state in which managers, individuals, units, and departments use their collaborative power in their working relationships to accomplish a common goal for the organization. They combine their resources to achieve these results by using their power cooperatively with others, having a positive attitude toward themselves and others, accepting differences in people and using these differences productively and collaboratively, and being open to the discovery of new ideas and approaches. When interdependence does not exist, people do not talk to each other; they blame, compete, conflict, avoid, resist, and greatly underutilize each other as resources.

One of the strong points of Japanese management philosophy is its emphasis on collective responsibility. The Japanese use work groups extensively, and managers are taught to be interdependent with others as integral parts of a larger human unit (Hatvany and Pucik, 1981). In the United States, individual responsibility, independence, and self-sufficiency are emphasized. There is often the feeling that if time is spent with others, the tasks will not get done. There is high task orientation, and little time is spent working with the human process of relationships and interdependence. Sometimes in the rush to finish things, managers make decisions without involving the people who have to carry them out and then find that the decisions are not implemented successfully. The Japanese spend large amounts of time in their decision-making process, resisting closure until everyone sees what is required and clearly understands their part in implementing the decision. Consequently, interdependence is a way of life in many Japanese organizations and is constantly being reinforced.

When there is teamwork, there is interdependence. However, interdependence is more than teamwork. When managers are working interdependently, they are using the concept in their managing and relating it to the total organization. There are times when they need to work interdependently with other managers on an occasional basis, in problem-solving groups or special-project task forces that are disbanded after the project is completed. Teams are groups that have to work with each other in an ongoing relationship to accomplish common goals. Managers who are working interdependently are highly aware that their actions and decisions affect others. They are in contact with these people before making decisions that will affect them. Similarly, they are aware of the human resources in the larger organization and use them as needed—and expect to be used by other managers when they have a need.

Why Interdependence Is Important

When individuals, units, and departments work together interdependently, there is less competitiveness and more focus on and commitment to the mission of the organization. There are fewer surprises of the type that occur when one unit does something that has an adverse effect on the operation of another. Consequently, there are fewer "personality conflicts" be-

tween powerful individuals. These conflicts are usually role conflicts that come about because working relationships are not
clear and people are not expressing their wants to each other.
When interdependence is practiced, it is a basis for resolving
conflict because of the strong commitment to organization results. People are willing to do what is necessary to make it
happen.

Under interdependence, managers feel free to give to others without expecting anything in return, to receive without
feeling they have to give something back, to ask others for help
and what they need, and to refuse when appropriate without
rejecting someone personally. Peters and Waterman (1982)
point out that, in an excellent organization, people are constantly asking for help from others regardless of where they are
in the organization and get informal groups together to solve
problems. When this norm exists, there is strong motive for
learning in order to respond to others and operate jointly with
them. Different people know different parts of the problem and
bring diverse knowledge and expertise to problem solving, resulting in superior decisions and better working relationships.

Interdependence and Participation

When interdependence is the mode of using personal
power, there will necessarily be a high level of participation.
For successful participation to take place, managers must have
a Theory Y attitude toward people, rather than the authoritarian style that has been traditionally used in many organizations. At Graphic Controls, the participative style of leadership
was described as focusing on the responsibility of both individuals and groups, as compared with solely individual responsibility under the authoritarian style. There was the authority
of knowledge instead of the authority of power. Managers
shared power instead of using power to coerce people into performing. Conflict and confrontation were discussed and differences resolved instead of being avoided or used destructively.
There was interdependence instead of independence. Feedback
was two way rather than merely downward. Lastly, there was

active, effective listening in the participative style, as compared with poor listening skills under the authoritarian style (Miller, 1980). Real participation produces a high level of internalized commitment, whereas, under the authoritarian style, orders (decisions) command commitment. This is the difference between self-control by employees toward objectives to which they are committed and external control and threat of punishment to achieve objectives.

Power is a big issue in changing from the authoritarian style to the participative style. A manager using positive practices will see power as coming from the person rather than from the hierarchical position, as in the traditional view. Rubin and Berlew say that "leaders who resist the instinct to manage more tightly during difficult times and instead support the personal power and entrepreneurship of their middle managers create an organizational culture that bonds powerful people together in pursuit of a common goal—like a flock of wild geese flying in perfect V-shaped formation" (Rubin and Berlew, 1984, p. 35).

It is difficult for a manager with an authoritarian style to change to a participative style. It is particularly hard to share power, listen, and receive feedback, some of which the manager may not like. It is also hard for some managers to shift from individual responsibility to a combination of individual and group responsibility. We find that it is helpful for managers who wish to change to look at their own identity and attitude toward themselves, as discussed in Chapter Eleven. How counseling may also be useful is described in Chapter Twelve.

Using Personal Power Interdependently

The four power styles that determine how a manager uses personal power are dependent, counterdependent, independent, and interdependent. If the interdependent mode is not the predominant one, personal power will be used dysfunctionally. There will be negative games, and people will limit themselves to their functional areas rather than thinking organizationally. Each of the four power modes is appropriate in certain situations, but interdependence has to be the predominant one. A summary of the characteristics of these four power styles is given in Table 1. The complete description will be found in "The Development of Power Relationships in Management" by John C. Talbot in *Making MBO/R Work* (Beck and Hillmar, 1976, p. 56).

For a manager to change to interdependence as his or her basic style is a major change, similar to that of changing from an authoritarian to a participative style. A key to this change is for the manager to be clear about his or her identity. The manager needs to (1) be aware of his or her personal power (potency), (2) be clear about what he or she values and needs, (3) have self-assurance, (4) be willing and able to let go, and (5) be capable of intimacy—sharing oneself with others.

A manager who has adopted the interdependent style as the preferred one is willing to ask for what he or she wants, to relate to others, to say and accept "no," to accept polarities, to tolerate ambiguity, and to feel that it is all right to be a part of the group without having to dominate. These behaviors are similar to those of the "I am OK with me—you are OK with me" life position of transactional analysis. In this position, the manager is using his or her power with others to achieve what is good for the organization and the individuals involved.

Intimacy

As intimacy is such an important element in the interdependence power style, misconceptions about this word need to be clarified. In *Intimate Marriage,* the Clinebells (Clinebell and Clinebell, 1970) describe a dozen ways that one can have intimacy with others. Some of the areas where intimacy is possible are emotions, intellectuality, esthetics, creativity, recreation, work, crisis, commitment, spirituality, and sex. The trap that many fall into is assuming that sex and intimacy are synonymous. The Clinebells point out that a couple can have sex without intimacy. Emotional intimacy occurs when there is a deep sharing of significant meanings and feelings. Intellectual intimacy can be experienced in the closeness resulting from sharing ideas and experiencing development of new concepts. Cre-

Table 1. Four Power Styles.

	Dependent	Counterdependent	Independent	Interdependent
Work	Tell me what you want. Do this for me.	Whatever you're for, I'll resist it—or at least have reservations. That's not enough.	This is where it's at for me—where are you?	I want from you. . . . What do you want from me?
Norms	I'll do anything to please you. Show me, please.	Try and show me. Don't do that anymore. Enough is never enough. I can do it all by myself.	I'll do my thing. You do your thing.	Let it be. . . . Mutual give-receive. Discovery is more important than invention.
Attitudes	Please accept me, feed me, take care of me. You *must* take care of me.	I'll resist you, but I'm not sure I want to be responsible for my own actions. I still like the shelter of dependency.	It's important for me to stand on my own. Only I can be responsible for my actions.	I can be me, and you can be you. Our differences are important.
Power	I get power from you.	I resist power in others to find how my power is different (better than) others'.	I use my power to assert my uniqueness.	We both have power. I join my power with your power to do things that matter.
Uses	Utilizing external or different resources.	Testing reality, workability. Extending self, influence, boundary, power.	Exercising initiative. Maintaining boundaries or autonomy.	Collaboration in work. Appreciation and valuing.
Misuses	Not using own power. Playing it safe, coasting, free-loading.	Blocking, inhibiting, fighting, or withholding that cancels out other's efforts.	Isolated, disruptive unilateral actions. Undercommunicating. Ignoring accountability.	Hidden dependency. "Masking." Leaning on other people.
Relations	You win—I win. You lose—I lose. I'm not OK. You're OK.	You win—I lose. You lose—I win. I'm OK? You're OK?	I win. Indifference. I'm OK. You're OK?	I win—you win. You win—I win. I'm OK. You're OK.

Source: Adapted from Beck and Hillmar, 1976, p. 56. Used by permission.

ative intimacy comes from shared creativity—the closeness that is felt when we have a major breakthrough in solving a seemingly unsolvable problem. Recreational intimacy may occur during hiking, backpacking, or an exciting game of tennis, golf, basketball, or soccer. Work intimacy may result from the closeness, physical and mental, of working together on a project. The mutuality that stems from a job well done is an added bonus of work intimacy. Crisis intimacy occurs when people have to come together to handle a crisis. Foresters talk about the intimacy that develops when fighting a fire for several days; soldiers talk about the intimacy in the trenches. Work teams experience it when they work day and night to meet a special customer need.

Some people were raised in homes where there was little or no intimacy. A child raised in this environment may make the decision not to get close to others, not to touch others, and not to share feelings. Managers who have had this experience may resist getting close to others and developing intimacy in the workplace. To change this decision and reduce the resistance, it may be necessary to get the help of a competent therapist. People who are able to make this breakthrough find that it is an exhilarating experience without sexual implications and that it can happen anywhere. When this happens in the workplace, the results may be phenomenal for both the organization and the individual. Synergy takes place, and, somehow, two plus two equals five or sometimes even seven.

Intimacy occurs when you are able to satisfy your social needs in direct response to those of another human being. You are able to make good contact with others. According to Herman and Korenich (1977, pp. 57-58), contact is

> when two people are really seeing, hearing and experiencing each other and what is going on *right here, right now.* There is minimum interference with your sensing processes. When you are not in good contact, your senses are being interfered with —you are worrying, thinking of something other than what is going on here and now; making as-

sumptions in your mind about what the effects of your words will have on the other person, and so on. When your mind is preoccupied, it is unlikely that you are really able to use your eyes and ears to experience what is really happening in your immediate situation. The persons conversing are involved with one another and the conversation contains excitement, presence and liveliness. Signs of poor contact include boredom, impersonal discussion, a droning voice, talking about others, the distant past or the far future.

There is trust, empathy, openness, truth, and risk taking. You are able to accept vulnerability and what comes with it, and you are also able to fight, to conflict, and to confront fully. Dominance does not exist, and you do not have to be competitive. You are able to build highly productive relationships that are good for you, others, and the organization as a whole.

Personality Types

It is easier to talk about relationships than to actually build productive ones. We have found that Jungian psychology on personality types provides a helpful structure for understanding the differences and similarities among human beings. An understanding of your personality type increases your awareness of how you prefer interacting with others and how you function in making decisions and securing information. The Myers-Briggs Type Indicator (MBTI) is a simple and reliable instrument to develop this awareness. The MBTI was developed by Isabel Briggs Myers for the main purpose of making some of the principles of Jungian psychology available to people in order to improve their relationships in life, to grow and develop, and to achieve balance in the way they operate and relate to others.

The MBTI helps managers and team members identify their preferences for extraversion or introversion. When this is known, managers will understand why some people like being in groups and others do not. Introverts usually will not speak up in a group unless they are asked for opinions or feel very comfortable in that group. Extraverts have no problem speaking up and may very easily dominate discussions. It has been found that 75 percent of our society prefer extraversion and 25 percent introversion.

The second pair of personality preferences in the MBTI is sensing and intuition. These are ways of perceiving things and getting information. These two preferences are probably the source of most miscommunication and misunderstanding. People who prefer sensing tend to value experience and the wisdom of the past and want to be realistic, practical, factual, and sensible. Those who prefer intuition tend to value hunches, a vision of the future, speculation, possibilities, ingenuity, and imagination. This is not to say that persons who prefer sensing do not have hunches, but they usually do not pay attention to them. Approximately 75 percent of the population prefer sensing and 25 percent intuition.

The third pair, thinking and feeling, describes preferences for the basis on which to make decisions. Thinking types are more comfortable with impersonal, objective judgments, whereas feeling types prefer personal value judgments. Those who prefer impersonal choice respond positively to words such as *objectives, principles, policy, firmness,* and *criticism.* The feeling types react positively to words such as *subjective, values, extenuating circumstances, intimacy,* and *persuasion.* While the total population is evenly divided on this combination, six out of ten men prefer thinking, and six out of ten women prefer feeling. This is the only case of a difference in preference by sex.

The fourth pair of personality preferences is judging and perceiving. These two describe a person's attitude or preference regarding closure versus keeping things open and fluid. The judging types prefer words such as *decided, settled, planning, schedules, closure,* and *deadlines,* and they might be heard saying "Let's wrap it up" or "Get the show on the road." Perceiving types like expressions such as *pending, gather more data, flexible, adapt as you go, spontaneous, keep options open,* and *emergent,* and they will say things such as "Let's wait and see."

When managers are aware of their personality types, they are aware of what is behind their behavior—the strength of their drive and also the pitfalls. For instance, a manager with a high judging preference will have no difficulty making decisions but may make them too fast, whereas a manager with a high perceiving preference may have difficulty making decisions but will insist on getting adequate facts before making them. When a manager and his or her team are aware of this, they can use both strengths to achieve balance in making good decisions.

Another example of the use of personality preferences is the need for balance between thinking and feeling types. Those with a preference for basing decisions on the thinking, rational, logical approach will be very objective. On the other hand, the feeling type, who is more likely to be people oriented, will be more subjective in the decision-making process and may ignore the logical or rational aspects of the situation. In organizations dominated by thinking types, decisions are often made without consideration for people's feelings. In these cases, good decisions may be sabotaged intentionally or unintentionally, and there is usually poor morale. Using the MBTI enables a manager to be sure that all eight personality preferences are used in balance in the organization. The MBTI can also have a significant impact on managers and teams in understanding themselves and others, accepting themselves and others positively, and increasing their awareness that at times it is appropriate to behave in ways that conflict with their preferred way.

This summary of MBTI and Jungian psychology was taken from *Please Understand Me* (Keirsey and Bates, 1978) and *Gifts Differing* (Myers and Myers, 1980). Both are recommended reading for those interested in exploring this concept in depth.

Teamwork as a Part of Interdependence

One way for a manager to build interdependence is to emphasize teamwork in his or her unit and seek teamwork at his or her level in the organization. Teams are groups of individuals who must work interdependently, at least at times, in order to accomplish their tasks and may make decisions as a group. Managers must be clear with their teams on their role in decision making. In some areas, they may make decisions and then announce them to the team. They may consult with the team on some decisions or use the consensus method, joining with them in making certain decisions. The more involvement that a manager allows the team in this process, the higher will be his or her utilization of the group's resources and the higher the level of trust.

Athletic teams are good examples of the need for interdependence. The members have a common purpose and goal, and each member has a unique function (position) that must be integrated with that of other members. The players are aware and supportive of the need for interdependent interaction (Karp, 1980). We often see a basketball team that is playing as a team beat a group with more talent but with each player acting as an individual star. In basketball, the difference is between the team with a common goal of putting the ball in the basket and beating the opponents and the group whose players are more concerned with their own scoring than with supporting the team member who has the best opportunity to score. The organizational parallel to the winning team is the group whose members think organization first and their individual jobs second. This may mean at times giving up some "turf" to improve organizational achievement.

To build a team, a manager has to focus on the covert problems, the social and emotional needs of the members of the team, as well as the overt problems of getting the job done. The manager should insist that the group be constantly aware of and evaluating the process of how they are working together. Some of the process items to evaluate are how straight (honest) and open team members are with each other, their willingness to disagree and express their feelings to each other, their willingness to give feedback, both positive and negative, to each other, and their willingness to support and hold each other accountable.

For the team concept to work, the manager of the team must have a participative style. Though he or she may be directive when appropriate, the manager must constantly work toward shared responsibility and development of individual skills. Bradford and Cohen (1984b) describe this type leader as the "manager-as-developer," as distinguished from the "heroic" leader who can know all, do all, and solve every problem. The leader must hold the team accountable for solving problems together and being cooperative and include their performance in these areas in their performance appraisals. It may be necessary to be directive at times, telling them "I expect you to solve this problem together. If you have difficulty doing this, I will help or get you consulting help if necessary. You have to learn how to solve problems together."

Team building is an ongoing process. In the early stages, it usually requires outside consulting help until the manager and team members develop the necessary skills to handle the communication problems that will occur. The manager may require consulting help him- or herself if he or she is changing from a directive style to a participative style of leadership. The primary item in the team-building process is the building of trust.

Building Trust

Trust is the essential ingredient in the developing of interdependent relationships. Our daily lives are built on trust. We trust that other motorists will obey traffic signals, that stores will honor our currency, that services such as water, gas, and electricity are available when we need them, and so on. Our coins and paper money bear the words "In God We Trust." Despite this, we quite often have a low level of trust in our organizations. Trust is based on repetitive transactions yielding consistent results, and it begins with an initial period of reaching out to others. To develop trust in a unit, a manager has to be consistent and start with his or her own willingness to trust others.

The manager has to allow subordinates to make decisions and must delegate tasks to them. It is essential that he or she support them in their decision making and at the same time hold them accountable. This development of subordinate decision making usually requires training and coaching on the part of the manager. It also requires the manager to be clear with subordinates on expectations, results desired, limits and boundaries to decision-making authority, and when and in what form reports are required from them. The way a manager handles mistakes and failures is crucial, because a subordinate who is punished will be reluctant to make more decisions. When there is failure, some questions the manager may ask the subordinate are: "What happened?" "Was there something you needed that you did not get?" "What were the alternatives you had?" "How might you have handled this situation differently?" "What will you do to prevent this in the future?" (Other suggested approaches are found in Chapter Seven.) After exploring the situation with the subordinate, the manager may supportively say: "Even though this decision did not work out well, I do like your willingness to make the decision."

Shea (1984) provided a positive way of handling a failure that occurred at General Electric. A special project team had developed a 5,000-hour light bulb, but it failed in the marketplace after the energy crisis of the late 1970s abated. Even so, Welch, the chief executive officer, recognized the team's efforts with a party, gifts, and promotions for some. This was a strong message from management that it is all right to take risks and "fail"; that is, that developmental teams should not be punished for unpredictable marketplace fluctuations. A comment about Welch described him as not being afraid to be wrong. You do not punish people for honest mistakes as long as they did the best they could.

Some of the behaviors that destroy trust are judgments that are based on prejudice, anger, or retribution; controlling behavior; manipulative strategies; neutral behavior, as opposed to empathy; being distant; and being absolutely certain rather than provisional. A manager who is using any of these destructive behaviors and wishes to change needs to talk to subordinates about this behavior and ask them and others close to him or her to point it out when it occurs. The use of support groups is helpful to managers wishing to change behavior.

Support Groups

A support group is a type of interdependent relationship where people can share problems and feelings and be vulnerable without fear that what they say will be used against them or that they will be judged. It is a group where people receive positive strokes on their progress toward their goals and where they will be confronted when they are not carrying out their commitments and have lapsed into old behavior that they wish to change. Examples of strong support groups in our society are Alcoholics Anonymous and Weight Watchers. People generally accomplish their goals, whether abstinence from alcohol or lower weight, while they are committed to the support group, but they quite often revert to their old behavior when they drop out of their support group and do not replace it with another, similar group. Support groups can be used by a manager who wishes to make a behavior change to any of the positive practices mentioned in this book.

These groups can start with two people and grow to a maximum size of twelve. A loan teller in a branch bank related an incident where she and a colleague decided they needed to do something about the stress that they felt on Fridays, when they had many customers and problems and were open until 7:00 P.M. They decided to have breakfast together every Friday and get themselves into a positive frame of mind for the stressful day and invited all the other employees of the branch to join them. Although the others initially declined, a few employees gradually joined them until, after two months, every employee of the branch breakfasted together. They also started potluck lunches on Friday, when they usually did not have time to go out for lunch. Friday became a fun day in the branch. Even the customers felt the lessening of tension as the stressful situations were handled positively. When the loan teller was later transferred, as were the branch manager and several others, the Friday breakfasts and potlucks stopped. As the teller related, "The attitude in that branch is awful now. I hate to even go in there." This is an example of working interdependence, people using their power together to achieve a desired change.

When asked "How can I change a group of which I am a member that enjoys putting down anyone who makes a mistake, but seldom praises?", Odiorne (1984, p. 4) responded: "Don't try to change things just after you have been ravaged and ridiculed, or it will seem that you are just being defensive and you'll be pounded just that much harder. Rather, find someone who has just been victimized and get that person to agree that the two of you together will try to change the behavior of the group. Then you can quietly approach others one at a time to ask: 'Why do we always seem to be knocking one another when we should be supporting each other?' You don't have to have a majority to swing a group, just two or three determined people who assume some leadership."

Some of the characteristics of support groups are as follows (adapted from Allen and Kraft, 1982):

1. Membership: two or more, maximum of twelve; voluntary; people added slowly; OK to leave group.
2. Support for change—common goals.
3. Democratic—participatory in decision making.
4. Self-led or led by facilitator.
5. Atmosphere: trust (safe), nonblaming, nonjudgmental, acceptance of differences, sharing, commitment, confronting in a caring way, and caring relationships.
6. Clarity on goals and purpose.
7. Focus on results rather than activities and promises.
8. Feedback given and received.
9. Negative norms confronted, not people.
10. Positive behavior reinforced.
11. Sustained commitment—follow-through.
12. Provision for renewal.

Interdependence in Japanese Management

To see the effect of interdependence on productivity, we can take a look at management in many Japanese organizations. The Japanese have a devotion to human assets and develop their management system so that the elements are interdependent and reinforce each other. One of their strategies to accomplish that is developing their people as generalists through slow promotion, job rotation, and internal training, thereby promoting good communications across functional areas. In their complex appraisal system, evaluation includes not only the bottom line but also personality traits and behaviors, such as creativity, emotional maturity, and cooperation with others, as well as team performance results.

Another strategy is the assigning of tasks to work groups, rather than individuals, with attention to structural factors that enhance motivation and cooperation. Group autonomy is encouraged by avoidance of reliance on experts to solve operational problems. Managers and supervisors also spend a large percentage of their time with their employees and rely considerably on consultative decision making. Much time is spent involving those who have to implement the decision in the decision-making process. While this process is time consuming, it reduces anxiety and the time to implement the decision (of course, when time is short, the manager in charge makes the decision). Managers need to be evaluated on the quality of their relationships with their subordinates (Hatvany and Pucik, 1981).

Achieving interdependence often requires a major change in a manager's attitude toward him- or herself and others. One of the aspects of achieving this desired change is a commitment to personal growth. The next three chapters are devoted to positive practices that managers can use in their own development and can encourage their associates to use.

⚔ 11 ⚔

Overcoming
Internal Barriers
to Success

⚔ ⚔ ⚔ ⚔ ⚔ ⚔ ⚔ ⚔

We read about a pediatrician telling a young mother, "If you do not take care of yourself, you will not have the energy to take care of your baby." There is only so much energy. If we do not replenish ours, we will not have any to give to others. We must be free to receive and ask for help at all times. Otherwise, we are in danger of eventual burnout. Ask yourself who is the most important person in your life. The answer should be "I am!" If it is spouse, child, parent, mentor, or someone else, you are putting that person ahead of you and, therefore, probably not taking care of yourself adequately. For some, it will sound selfish to put oneself before loved ones. However, if you look at it from the standpoint that you must have good energy if you are to give to others, it is easier to accept the need to take care of yourself. This is part of empowering yourself to use your potency and energy in problem solving.

It is easy to think of yourself in roles—parent, son, sister, or wife at home and accountant, manager, salesperson, or programmer at work. When you do that, you do not see yourself as a human being. You are more than your role: you are a person, a human being, first. Acceptance of this gives you permission to be clear about your identity and to constantly work to discover all the good things about yourself that you have covered up or denied over the years.

This chapter will concentrate on how managers can get clear with themselves about their persons. These positive practices are helpful to managers in building their own self-esteem and self-confidence and overcoming fears and insecurity. In using these positive practices themselves, they will be more aware of how they can help others in these areas. By getting clear with themselves, they also will be better able to use the other positive practices offered in this book.

This is a highly personal subject and somewhat difficult to write about, as it works differently for each of us. The best way we know is to share our own experiences and the experiences of others to give you some idea of how to go about changing your attitude about yourself. You, the manager, will have to learn to use whatever works for you. When you make human resources a top priority, you will see the need to deal with personal issues. There will be high emphasis on people growing and developing as human beings as well as managers, technicians, and operators. We believe that one of the basic problems keeping a manager from managing well is insecurity from low self-worth. Where there is insecurity, some managers may put up a strong front to mask a low self-image. Others may behave very passively, avoiding evaluation and confrontation. There will probably be defensiveness, blaming, criticizing, avoidance, or other destructive behavior.

Behavioral Aspects of a Clear Identity

When you are clear on your identity as a human being, you will be aware of your needs and wants and be willing to ask to get them satisfied. You can also accept your uniqueness and your values and know the reasons behind your behavior. With this awareness, you are better able to look at the behavioral choices you have in situations. When you are aware that you make choices, consciously or unconsciously, you will take responsibility for yourself and your behavior. No one can make you angry; you choose whether to be angry when someone does something to you. Consequently, you say not "You made me angry" but "When you behave that way, I get angry, and I will appreciate your stopping it." There is no blaming in the latter statement; you are asking for what you want. The other person will usually oblige or move into problem solving to lessen the unwanted behavior. Another statement that is disempowering and denies choices is "I can't do that." When you ask yourself, "Who is stopping me?", you discover that, in most instances, the person is yourself. Consequently, the straight, responsible statement is "I won't do that" or "I choose not to do that." Such statements put you in a position to look at your choices and the risks involved. On that basis, you then make a conscious decision on the action to be taken.

Clarity on identity results in a high degree of spontaneity and creativity. When you are sure of yourself and willing to share your ideas and thoughts with others, even though you may not always be able to explain them logically, you are listening to your intuition. Also, when you are clear on your identity, you are able to communicate with others with the minimum of defensiveness and blaming. You are also able and willing to develop intimate relationships with others. The closeness and good feelings result in positive and more productive working relationships. You are able to make contact with others more readily and let go of them when appropriate. Finally, you are aware of your technical and managerial competence and willing to use it freely and productively. You are willing to take risks in your organization and in your personal life to achieve improvement and development. This means that you are willing to explore new ways and new insights and are open to discovery and the ideas, suggestions, and feedback of others without feeling threatened. You are open to your own intuition and not dependent exclusively on external data. There is balance in the way you are managing and living your life.

How You Got the Way You Are

Psychologists say that we make most of the decisions on how we live our lives before we are six years old. We were influenced by the social environment in which we lived and by the authority figures in our lives—parents, grandparents, uncles and aunts, older brothers and sisters, ministers and priests, teachers, and so on. Sometimes we blame our parents and others for the way we are. It is important that we accept the fact that we made the decisions on our lives, some consciously and some unconsciously. We made these decisions in order to survive, and they were probably appropriate at that time; we did the best that we knew how. Some of us decided to be like our parents, and some decided to be different. An example is twin boys who had an alcoholic father. At age twenty-one, one of the twins was an alcoholic and the other was a teetotaler.

We learn how to survive. For instance, we know a person who experienced violence in his family when he was a small child and learned how to withdraw and ignore it. This same behavior is still with him at times today. When there is uncomfortable conflict, his first response is to withdraw and avoid it. Now that he is aware of this pattern, he deliberately changes his behavior and deals with the conflict. He also asks for feedback from colleagues and his family when they see him in his avoidance behavior, which is dysfunctional in his organization and with his family.

These early decisions in life are basically centered around our self-worth or, in transactional-analysis language, "my OKness with me." We may decide that we are OK in some ways and not OK in other ways—for example, that we have book sense but not common sense. This decision may result in our making top grades in school but poor decisions in our life situations. Other not-OK decisions might be that we are not creative or not good at mathematics. Living with these decisions will result in a negative attitude about creativity and problem solving and difficulty with mathematics or financial concerns.

When we accept responsibility for the decisions that we have made about how to live our lives, we have taken the first step toward change. We can change any of these decisions at any time. Of course, some will be more difficult and painful to change than others, and we may need a good therapist to help us. We can then start a new pattern of responsive behavior. This change can happen by a conscious, deliberate act of will.

Ways to Determine Self-Worth

You need both self-analysis and help from others to determine whether your behavior shows evidence of low self-worth in these areas (adapted from Osborne, 1976, pp. 55–66):

1. Being overly sensitive—your response to being confronted and receiving negative feedback from others. Do you become defensive and angry, or do you withdraw?
2. Being excessively argumentative, to prove a point. Do you have a win-lose attitude?
3. Being critical of others. Are you aware that often what you criticize in others is what you dislike in yourself?
4. Being intolerant of others and their ideas. Do you see them as threats, or do you think that only you have good ideas?
5. Being a hostile person. Do you project your anger onto others? Do you fly off the handle at the least provocation?
6. Wanting to punish others. Are you forgiving of others, and do you free yourself from the need to get back at those who have done something to you?
7. Not listening to others. Do you ignore others or think of something else while they are talking?
8. Being overly materialistic. Are you concerned only with materialism and not sensitive to the human and feeling aspects of situations? The opposite of this may also be a problem.
9. Being insecure and fearful. Do you allow your insecurity and fear to block your humanness toward others?
10. Putting undue emphasis on status symbols. Do you allow the desire for titles, degrees, and honors to get in the way of being human?
11. Knowing what to do when you lose. Are you hostile or depressed when you lose or things go against you?
12. Having difficulty receiving compliments. Do you feel that you are not worthy of compliments or that you should have done better, that you never do enough?

This checklist helps you determine your self-worth and whether you are spending your time in the positive OK position. These are areas where you place handicaps on yourself in playing the game of life. You can look at your life as a game of tennis, where your goal is getting the ball over the net as often as possible—not winning but keeping on playing. When you have high self-worth, you are not easily defeated.

The Disadvantages of Low Self-Worth

Low self-worth brings with it many disadvantages and barriers to top performance. It is the self-fulfilling prophecy—when you expect and feel the negative, that is usually what will happen. You prove you are correct in your perception and feelings. Low self-worth—not-OK life position—results in negative behavior and a negative environment. This gives rise to insecurity, hostility, depression, and many barriers to problem solving and productivity, both individually and organizationally. There are feelings of inferiority and superiority. There are many negative "shoulds" that prevent individuals and groups from being free to use their competency in contributing to organizational achievement.

Those with the insecurity of the "I am not OK" position will wait for someone else to take the lead. They will probably be obsessed with the past and have considerable fear of such things as making a mistake, failure, rejection, the unknown, or not being able to handle the results of their actions. People with such fears are not free to be themselves and have handicaps in being productive. They are constantly trying to prove themselves to others. They are defensive, worrying, and blaming and spend their time and energy in "CYA" ("cover your behind") and survival efforts.

Guilt occurs in the "I am not OK" position. If the inner self is pursuing incompatible goals, there is a vague, gnawing sense of remorse, uneasiness, or anxiety when both goals cannot be achieved. Failure to "do right," be perfect, or complete a project may bring on guilt. Violating a negative "should" is the cause for many of their splits in goals. Fifteen minutes is long enough to feel guilt about anything. Either rectify the error or forgive yourself, or both, and move on. If you continue to feel guilty, this negativity will sap your energy, and there will be little or nothing to give to others and the organization.

The Value of High Self-Worth

High self-worth contributes to a positive attitude and makes people hopeful and confident that they can achieve for themselves while they are achieving for the organization. When people are in this state, they are more spontaneous and responsive to their intuitions. They feel more secure in themselves and are willing to take more risks and feel free to accept help from others without being threatened. They grow, develop, and increase their contributions to their organizations. They are excited and energized by the discovery of their many talents and good points. They take control of their lives, aware of the choices that they have, and deliberately make decisions about their lives.

When all of these characteristics are present, a person is living the "being" values identified by Maslow (1968) in his description of the state of self-actualization: wholeness, perfection, completion, justice, aliveness, richness, simplicity, beauty, goodness, uniqueness, effortlessness, playfulness, truth, and self-sufficiency. When managers and their subordinates feel this way, the organization will have available the whole human resource, and the needs of the organization and the individuals will be satisfied.

How to Get Clear on Your Identity

In getting clear about yourself, you will be clear on your identity. You will know who you are, your values, your biases and prejudices, your strengths and weaknesses, and how all of these fit together to make you an "OK" human being. To achieve and maintain this clarity, you have to work constantly to develop the necessary self-discipline. It is well to remember that there are "no free lunches." When you accept yourself as the most important person in your life, you will devote the necessary time, effort, and resources. Some things you can do alone; with others, you will need support from associates, friends, and family. Some of the tools and techniques that you can use are listed here:

1. Use silence to listen to your intuition and draw on your inner power source (see Chapter Thirteen). You will be pleasantly surprised with the solutions to problems that will come to you at these times.
2. Use affirmations and visualization to program your unconscious, as described in Chapter Thirteen, for positive experiences and achievement of goals.
3. Develop your own distinctive holistic stress-management program, as described in Chapter Twelve, to meet your individual needs.
4. Start or join a support group with others dedicated to the same goal that you wish to achieve, as discussed in Chapter Ten.
5. Attend personal-growth workshops that have objectives that are compatible with yours.
6. Read books such as *Be the Person You Were Meant to Be* (Greenwald, 1974) and others. There are a growing number of good books on the bookshelves today.
7. Use psychological tests designed to help you become aware of your values and personality preferences in making decisions. Ones we have found helpful are "Values for Working" (Flowers, Hughes, Myers, and Myers, 1975) and the Myers-Briggs Type Indicator (Myers and Myers, 1980). When you have this understanding of yourself, you are more aware of the choices you have in the way you behave and can choose to behave differently if what you are now doing is causing problems for others or not producing what you want.
8. Work to change negative norms in the organization to norms that are supportive of your goals (see Chapter Five).

Use all of these techniques to increase your awareness of yourself and why you behave, feel, and think the way you do. Of course, at times you will discover some things about yourself

that you do not like. It is important to accept your weaknesses
and negatives as well as your strengths and positives so that you
can accept yourself as a human being. You may also find that
the weaknesses or negatives may really be assets at times. We
find the following "five freedoms" articulated by Satir (1976,
p. 15) to be helpful: "to see and hear what is here instead of
what should be, was, or will be; . . . to say what one feels and
thinks instead of what one should; . . . to feel what one feels instead of what one ought; . . . to ask for what one wants instead
of always waiting for permission; . . . to take risks in one's own
behalf instead of choosing to be 'secure' and to not rock the
boat."

Discipline

To do all of this requires self-discipline. This means that
you have to maintain the self-control and orderliness to accomplish your goals. The word *discipline* does not appear very
often in management or personality literature, and it when
does, it usually refers to disciplining someone else—subordinates
or children. Peck (1978), in *The Road Less Traveled,* emphasizes the need for discipline, which he defines as "the means of
experiencing the pain of problems constructively." He gives
four tools for disciplining yourself: (1) delayed gratification, (2)
acceptance of responsibility, (3) dedication to the truth, and (4)
balancing.

Delayed Gratification. This is a process of scheduling
the painful or disliked tasks first and then experiencing the
things you like, the pleasurable things. Some children do this by
saving the best part of the cake—the icing—for last. This is applied in time management by doing the distasteful things before
doing the things you like to do. This discipline is helpful in
scheduling exercise and meditation at the same time each day.
It also works well when you have a disagreeable item to discuss
with a subordinate. When you perform the painful task first,
you will do it expeditiously and well.

Acceptance of Responsibility. You must accept responsibility for a problem before you can solve it. If you have a feel-

ing of self-worth, you are willing to accept responsibility for your decisions on how to live your life. Some of these decisions were made when you were a child and were appropriate for your survival but may not be appropriate today. When you take responsibility for this, you can make a deliberate decision to change your behavior so that you can be more positive and productive in your relationships.

Dedication to the Truth. When you are dedicated to the truth, you will endure the pain of self-examination. You will be open to challenges from others and willing to change your behavior when it is dysfunctional. Lying avoids the pain of challenge and circumvents legitimate suffering. We remember advice from Scott Myers, a management consultant: "When in doubt, be honest." Recently, a lawyer specializing in equal employment opportunity cases advised his client, "Always be honest with your employees, because if you are not, you will be found out, and then you are in deep trouble." Being truthful does not mean total openness, as it is appropriate at times to limit the revelation.

Balancing. Discipline is a demanding and complex task involving flexibility and judgment. Balancing is the discipline that gives you flexibility. An example of this is deciding whether to express anger. If you express it, you must do it in a nondestructive manner and not attack anyone's self-esteem. If you decide not to express it, you must use another way of diffusing it so that you do not dump it on someone else later or do harm to yourself. When you do not handle such things as anger, you will get out of balance, losing mental and emotional equilibrium.

Peck (1978) states that balancing is a discipline because the act of giving up something is painful. As you move through life, you must continually give up parts of yourself. This is applicable in organizations, as you may have to give up some things you cherish so that the organization is successful. You may even have to accept less achievement in your area in order not to disrupt other units.

We have experienced another example of balancing in our understanding of our personality types through the use of the Myers-Briggs Type Indicator (described in Chapter Ten). Now that we are aware of our personality preferences, we find that when we insist on behaving the way we like to behave, we may cause problems. We now know that we are capable of behaving in a different way, a way that is supportive of developing productive relationships and keeping things in balance. For instance, we may have a strong preference for making decisions quickly and sticking to schedules. Sometimes this causes problems, as we may push to make the decision prematurely, without sufficient information. Fortunately, we have some people around us who slow us down, and then we realize that we need to take more time to get more information. The decision is usually a better one.

Having a Confidant

When a manager—or any person—embarks on this journey, it is desirable to have a confidant, a person with whom you can be vulnerable, let your hair down, and admit your weaknesses and concerns without fear of your admissions being used against you. Preferably, the confidant should be a competent counselor, therapist, or consultant working with the organization; there may be more than one person. To facilitate change, a manager will also need a consultant who will give feedback on all aspects of his or her behavior in the organization as well as help make contracts with subordinates and colleagues. Above all, the manager must receive this feedback and use it. If the manager initially rejects the feedback, he or she should apologize when the damaged ego has healed.

Changes discussed in this chapter do not occur overnight. They require a long journey with many painful moments but many, many joyful and productive ones as well. It becomes easier the more you work at it and use the help that is available to you. The positive practices described in this chapter may be the first that a manager uses in embarking on a change in his or her management style, but they will be useful at any time in a manager's self-development. For further exploration of this topic see Huxley (1963), Osborne (1976), Satir (1978), Schwarz (1977), and Scott (1980).

12

Managing Stress Holistically

"Life without stress is life with no runs, no hits, no errors." So stated Selye (1974, p. 83), noted stress researcher. Positive stress causes us to get things done, to grow and develop. The negative aspects of stress are what can cause health problems and organizational performance problems. Up to a certain point, healthy tension is important to high performance. Beyond that point, fatigue can set in, followed by exhaustion, ill health, and perhaps even death. Our bodies can usually handle a high level of tension in the short range, but continued abuse over a long period of time will sap their necessary recuperative energy. This may lead to burnout and, ultimately, a breakdown if the stress is not relieved. When managers experience this continued high level of stress, they become irritable, negative, and depressed. This usually leads to hopelessness, helplessness, a negative environment, and a tendency to lose one's sense of purpose and do considerable complaining and blaming. As the individual becomes more fatigued and exhausted, there is increased absenteeism and reduced job performance.

When managers are managing with a positive attitude,

they are aware that what they are doing is good for them, their organization, and their customers or clients. They are able to cope with stress and avoid negativity and depression. In a positive environment, there is sensitivity to the stressful situations that individuals and groups experience, and efforts are made to help people deal with their stress in a positive way. Stress is cumulative, whether it is on the job or off the job. We cannot leave our personal problems at home. This chapter offers managers tools and techniques to handle stress effectively without negative effects on themselves and those around them, in the organization or in their families.

Stress and Its Causes

Stress, which has been called a twentieth-century disease, is a response to a stimulus, an uncomfortable condition that we experience when the body has created excess energy with which to defend itself. It is a direct consequence of how we define our personal relationship with the outer world. "Thus, the primary source of stress is not the external environment; it is the emotional and perceptual factors which form our basic personality" (Neurenberger, 1981, p. 8). Consequently, the response to the same stressor may vary from one person to another.

The internal response to a stressor speeds up the cardiovascular system and slows down the gastrointestinal function. Symptoms may include a quickening of the pulse, rapid breathing, nausea, pain in various parts of the body, constipation or diarrhea, headaches, inability to sleep or sleeping too much, dizziness, and so on. Shealy points out that the "most prominent reaction to emotional stress is an increased output of adrenalin and cortisone. Although both hormones are essential to life, in excess they race the body's functions and tend to wear it out. Blood pressure is elevated; the heart beats harder and more rapidly; blood salts are altered; kidneys are forced to work harder; the stomach produces more acidity and the entire intestinal tract may move sluggishly (or, alternatively, more rapidly and with irritation); circulation of blood in the skin is decreased; sweating increases; salivation is influenced; resistance to infections or cancer is reduced; susceptibility to allergies increases; and so on" (Shealy, 1976, p. 29).

When the stressor is removed, our bodies will return to normal unless a part of our body has been damaged. For instance, twenty years ago, John James moved his family to another city to take a new job. The stressors created were the move itself, getting the family settled, buying a house, selling the old house, commuting for several weeks, ending relationships, making new relationships, quitting one job, starting another, and so on. At the same time, his own and his wife's parents were ill. Then, when there were problems on the new job, his system became overloaded. He experienced dizziness, soreness of throat, pains in his chest, stomach cramps, colitis, and fluttering eyelids. Though he visited several doctors and received many tests, they could find nothing organically wrong with him. During that period, he took seven different tranquilizers. When he got another job back in his home city, the stressors were removed, and his health gradually returned to normal. According to the American Academy of Family Physicians (Wallis, 1983), two-thirds of the office visits to family doctors are prompted by stress-related symptoms. One doctor said his problem was determining which were psychosomatic and which were not.

The stressors, or stimuli, may be at work or away from work. They may be of short duration or long duration. The sources of stress usually fall into four categories: fear, overload or underload, life changes, and ambiguity. Feared physical or emotional harm could include ridicule, sarcasm, loss of love, or death—the actual leaving of this life, the end or breaking off of a relationship, or the loss of a job. We often imagine the worst happening in a situation that really is not so bad. Organizationally, the fear may be of failure and of the consequences. When managers are not getting adequate information on the status of their organization, their unit, or their own job, they might easily fear the unknown. There is usually fear associated with a new job, a new task, or the installation of a new system or technology. When adequate information is not passed out, the imagination runs wild, the negatives come through the grape vine, and there is a tendency to grab at the worst predictions. There is also fear associated with territoriality, where people are protective of their "turf" and responsibilities. Stress occurs when one person gets inside another's boundaries.

In the workplace, stress may be caused by too much work, continued overtime, or work that is too difficult or requires skills that one does not have. On the other hand, having little to do or a job that is not challenging can be stressful for some people. The stress can build to major proportions if there is no perceived way to relieve it. This may happen when a person is unwilling to ask for help or is denied help with the reply "That's your problem!" In some organizations, it is considered weakness to ask for help. However, we may be our own worst enemies here, if we are living by messages such as "I must do it all by myself," or "If you want it done right, you have to do it yourself."

Life changes that are stressful include the death of a spouse, which is considered the most stressful. Some remaining spouses never get over the loss, become ill, and may even die themselves shortly thereafter. Death of family members and close friends also rates high on the stress scale. Other stressful life changes are marital problems, separation and divorce, problems with children, financial problems, medical problems, children leaving home, birth of children, spouse going to work, and moving. We recently heard of a business executive who was transferred by his company three times, including a transcontinental move, in three years. Each move was a promotion, but it was disruptive for his wife and five young children. The family lived in four different houses in four different cities in three years. The stressors associated with relocating include leaving old and making new relationships, transferring schools, finding new doctors, buying and selling houses, living in motels, and so on. Unless this situation is managed well, the chance of illness, emotional problems, and low productivity is high. When there are problems at home, the stress is carried to the office or plant. Holmes and Rahe (1967) developed a rating scale of stressful events and weighted each. They found that the chance of an illness increased as the scores increased. Such events as death of spouse, divorce, and loss of job trigger other events, such as financial problems, moving, breaking relationships, and so on.

The fourth major category of stressors is ambiguity—the unknown, the unstructured, the uncertain, the unclear. Some ambiguity is normal, but much of it is caused by a lack of role clarification, being uncertain about what we are expected to do and not do. With such uncertainty, we do not know our rights, privileges, obligations, and authority to make decisions—our area of freedom—and we are unclear about potential consequences of our actions in carrying out our jobs. This includes the positive—the rewards and future with the organization—and the negative—discipline, demotion, or dismissal. Ambiguity stems from inadequate information on scope and responsibilities of the job, unclear objectives or none at all, and vagueness about what our boss and others expect from us. Role ambiguity leads to role conflicts, job-related tensions, feelings of futility, job dissatisfaction, underutilization, poor relations with boss, peers, and subordinates, inappropriate use of power, and physical anxiety.

Karasek (Wallis, 1983), an industrial-engineering professor at Columbia University, has found that people have higher rates of heart disease when they have little control over their jobs, high psychological demands, and little opportunity for independent decision making. This has been found with cooks, waitresses, cashiers, assembly-line workers, and telephone operators. Some people are more susceptible to stress problems than others. Cardiologists Friedman and Rosenman (1974) found that excessively aggressive-competitive "type A" personalities have a far higher risk of heart disease than a more integrated, balanced "type B" person. Type A people are constantly working against time, overscheduling, rushing to keep up, and exhibiting superhuman behavior. They cannot admit vulnerability to others, dislike warm feelings, and deny feelings in themselves. A type A manager will have to work harder to manage stress than will a type B manager.

An understanding of stress and how each of us responds to external stimuli is necessary to develop our awareness of the signals that we receive, individually and organizationally. When you are aware of the stress that you are putting on yourself and its negative effects on your health and well-being, you can decide whether you wish to change. When you take responsibility for what you do to yourself, you know that you can change your responses at any time and prepare yourself to cope effectively with the stressful events in your life.

Wellness

In working with stress management, we prefer to look beyond physical health, into wellness. The World Health Organization proposed that health be defined as a state of complete physical, mental, and social well-being, not merely the absence of disease or infirmity. This new approach is identified as *positive wellness*. It is a way of life—a life-style we design to achieve our highest potential for well-being (Travis, 1977). It involves our total being. People who enjoy positive wellness are trim and physically fit; full of energy, vigorous, rarely tired; free from minor complaints such as indigestion, constipation, headaches, and insomnia; alert, able to concentrate, clearheaded; radiant with clear skin, glossy hair, and sparkling eyes; active and creative; able to relax easily, free from worry and anxiety; self-assured, confident, optimistic; satisfied with work and the direction of their lives; able to assert themselves, stand up for their rights; satisfied with their sexual relationships; free from destructive health habits, particularly smoking, overeating, and excessive drinking; and fulfilled and at peace with themselves (Bloomfield and Kory, 1978).

We think that Maslow's (1968) "being" values, presented in Chapter Eleven, are characteristic of positive wellness. When you use positive practices, you strive for these conditions constantly. Though you probably will never attain them fully, you will achieve a level that gives you considerable satisfaction and a positive attitude. Our goal should be positive wellness: having hope while achieving laudable things for ourselves and our organizations.

Your Holistic Stress-Management Program

Keeping the goal of positive wellness in mind, you can develop your own holistic stress-management program. In the following section, we outline what we think such a program should include and some ideas for implementing yours. These are ideas that have worked for us and others; you can easily adapt them. Each person has to develop an individual program that meets his or her needs and is comfortable and enjoyable. We recommend evaluating what you are now doing. Keep the things that are working, change the things that are not working, and add new things. To adequately evaluate a new tool or technique, use it with awareness for at least thirty days before evaluating it.

Physical Aspects. The first part of a stress-management program will include exercise, breathing, rest, and nutrition. We recommend at least twenty minutes every other day of some form of strenuous exercise, such as running, swimming, bicycling, aerobics, or fast walking, to strengthen the cardiovascular system. Walking would require forty to sixty minutes for optimal results. Muscle-toning exercises, such as yoga, are recommended for strengthening muscles where stress may settle. For example, many of us experience tightness and pain in the upper back and shoulders when under tension. Neck, shoulder, and arm exercises both strengthen and relax these muscles. Massage is also helpful for relieving the tightness in these areas. Exercise increases energy and resistance to disease; it improves sleep, self-esteem, and self-confidence.

Breathing exercises are helpful for achieving deep breathing so that we take the necessary air into our bodies with the fewest breaths. When we are under tension, we tend to breathe shallowly and take many breaths, putting more strain on our cardiovascular system. Neurenberger (1981) provides some helpful hints on this subject. When feeling tension before an important meeting or giving a presentation, for example, a quick relaxing breathing exercise is slowly and easily taking ten deep breaths, filling the lungs while holding the abdomen flat and steady.

Adequate rest is essential to good stress management. It is

one of the best ways for relaxing and replenishing energy. As you grow older, you may need more sleep. But with a change in life-style to include more exercise, better nutrition, and better management of stress, you may find that you have more energy and need less sleep. Awareness of your needs is the key. For example, some people insist on getting a minimum of eight hours of sleep the night before a big event to assure that they are in the best possible condition.

What we eat has considerable influence on our health and our wellness. A change to a diet that is low in saturated fats, sugar, salt, and caffeine and high in fiber has been found to be helpful in curing some ailments. We know some people who have been cured of arthritis by a change in diet. Most of us consume more food than we need. Someone suggested to us that a way to remedy such overeating is to get up from the table a little hungry; you will discover later that you have had sufficient food. There are many tasty new recipes with low-calorie foods that can be substituted for high-calorie ones. These are some of the ways to get your weight to a level that is acceptable to you. There is also a place for vitamin supplements in your regular diet. We believe that nutrition is an individual matter, and each person has to find the combination of foods that is best for him or her. Consultation with physicians and nutritionists and reading various books on each subject will help in achieving all of this. After such consultation and research, each of us has to make our own decision on these choices.

Psychological Aspects. Some of the areas to work on psychologically are support systems, emotions, relationships, work, play, and psychotherapy. Many of these are covered in some detail in other parts of this book. Regardless of where you wish to start in a stress-management program, we recommend developing a support system of one or more people to work with you toward the same goal. Being complimented when we are doing well and confronted when we are not increases our commitment to a new program.

Awareness of our emotions and what is behind them helps us to control them so that they are not destructive of us or others. The first step is to accept that we determine our own emotions through our own choices. No one can make us angry or scared; we choose to respond with anger or fear in a particular situation. It is normal and natural to have emotions and feelings, and we will get angry or scared at times. Accepting and taking responsibility for our emotions will increase our awareness so that we can develop our own ways of diffusing them. Thus, minimum energy is expended, and they do not interfere with our communications and productivity. Relationships are also necessary in varying degrees for each of us. Developing and maintaining good relationships, at work and away from work, are important in achieving wellness.

We consider work under psychological aspects because we think it is necessary to enjoy our work. Work is an important part of our lives; if we dislike or dread it, we are increasing the stress on ourselves. Often we complain about our work and our organizations. Perhaps we even collude with others in this to develop many negative feelings. One way to reverse such behavior is to list all the positive things about our work and organization, as well as the negatives. Typically, the positives will far outweigh the negatives. What we want for ourselves from work is usually available to us, although getting it may mean negotiating new duties and responsibilities and exchanging some with others. If we continue doing the same thing year after year, most of us will become bored and burned out. Career planning is an important tool to keep work psychologically stimulating and energizing. Later in this chapter, we will discuss how organizations can be supportive of reducing stress at work.

Recreation and play are essential for relaxation and balance in our lives. Some of us who live by schedules and calendars have to schedule play times to be sure that we get this balance. We think that it is necessary to be careful in using competitive sports—tennis, handball, golf, and so on—for recreation, as they can create more stress. Some individuals' strong desire to win can make recreational sports another stressor. Competition is great when it is for fun and we are able to lose without being upset about it. Boating, sailing, fishing, and hiking are peaceful forms of recreation if they are not undertaken for the purpose of excelling. Other good forms might be dancing, the theater, or concerts. Again, each person must become aware of what form is best for him or her.

Another technique in this area is to treat yourself to a day of doing "nothing." You may find it both a creative and a relaxing day. You may have to start doing nothing fifteen minutes at a time, because you are remembering that old saying from your childhood: "Idle hands are the devil's playmates." Some of our parents were always busy, and some lived by the motto "Do this while you are resting." We now know that what an artist friend tells us is true: "A day of nothing is a highly creative day." Do whatever you want to do—sleep, read, walk in the woods, anything. You do not have to be productive or busy or constructive. The author of *The Road Less Traveled* (Peck, 1978) recently remarked that, including meditation, he does two hours of nothing each day. A day of nothing will be particularly difficult for type A personalities, but once they are able to accomplish it, it will probably be helpful for their temperament.

Psychotherapy is now being more widely accepted as a way for healthy people to get healthier. We have found it particularly helpful in getting through several traumatic events in recent years. It has been helpful in preventing illness when individuals have had high scores on the Holmes-Rahe scale of stressful life events. Good psychotherapists are facilitators in our discovery of self-worth. They are helpful in confronting and supporting when these are appropriate. We prefer therapists who use a holistic approach, dealing with body, mind, and spirit, and who are not totally dependent on a scientific model. Some of the things to look for in a therapist are an informal atmosphere, a good sense of humor, willingness to admit limitations and errors, and flexibility. You and the therapist should be comfortable with each other, and you should be made to feel that you are as worthy as the therapist.

We know some high-performance managers who use a counselor or therapist, though they usually do not tell anyone about it, since this positive use of such a resource is not widely accepted. They may use the therapist as a confidant—someone with whom they feel free to let their hair down and be vulnerable. Perham (1983) reports that many firms are turning to psychological consulting firms to counsel problem executives on their behavior in dealing with people. As an example of the profitability of this approach, for a $5,000 psychological counseling fee, a company was able to "salvage" a troubled executive who would have cost an estimated $100,000 to replace.

Spiritual Aspects. An essential element of a holistic stress-management program is working with the spiritual part of our being. Only recently has the word *spirituality* been used in the management literature, in some psychological publications, and in new approaches to health care. Naisbitt (1982) mentions that the spiritual needs of the workers, as well as the materialistic needs of technology, must be met. Similarly, *The Art of Japanese Management* (Pascale and Athos, 1981) discusses the place of spiritual values in organizations.

The spiritual dimension of our personality is the basis of our satisfaction or dissatisfaction with living. Spiritual health generates a sense of personal fulfillment, a sense of peace with self and the world. As we grow spiritually, we discover that we have the power to be self-fulfilling people, regardless of the problems and negatives around us. We also discover that the source of our fulfillment is within and experience an increased capacity to be alone, an ability to engage the issue of death, a realization of wholeness, and, ultimately, peace with ourselves (Bloomfield and Kory, 1978). When we achieve this state, we are better able to manage our stress effectively and stay in a positive position to work with others and solve problems.

Some of the tools and techniques that can help us to develop our spirituality are affirmations, visualization, and meditation (described in some detail in Chapter Thirteen). It is difficult, if not impossible, to explain how these tools work. We know that when we use them, we may get certain results, but there are no guarantees. Visualization and imagery techniques are now being used as part of treatment programs for some illnesses. An example of this is the work of the Simontons with cancer patients in Fort Worth and Dallas, Texas. There have been instances when ill people got well, defying the laws of science, which indicated that they should have died. The Simontons use visualization and imagery in conjunction with medical science and in most instances improve the quality of life while the patient is being treated (Simonton, Matthews-Simonton, and Creighton, 1978).

Achieving inner silence and calm is an objective in this area. We recently received feedback from a stress-seminar participant on how he handled stresses in his life the year after the seminar. "Personally, I have been through some very stressful situations during the past twelve months (three heart attacks in the family, two deaths, and a separation in my immediate family). Your sessions have helped, and I have often retreated to that special place to think restful, soothing thoughts. It's funny, but it's always the very same place, and I also greet most every new day with good feelings about myself and life in general." This is what happens when we program ourselves for positive experiences by deliberately changing our thought patterns and, as a result, changing our attitudes and expectations. Use of these tools and techniques can be the key to managing the stress in our lives effectively and helping maintain a positive attitude and work environment.

Other Tools and Techniques

We think that, in developing your own stress-management program, you should check out the ways that you are currently managing your stress effectively and use them more often. These include your life experiences, your support networks (people who nurture and console you), attitudes and beliefs that help protect you and help you view things differently, physical self-care habits that prepare you or help you to release tension, and other skills that you can use to change a stressful situation. You might review your career and life goals, delegate decisions, take a do-nothing day or a real vacation, get recognition and appreciation, or get training in areas that will help you in managing your job and your life.

To develop your own holistic stress-management program will necessitate some life-style changes. In order to make room for exercise, meditation, play, and so on, some activities may

have to be stopped or reduced. It may be necessary to change
your sleeping schedule, newspaper reading, TV watching, and
so on. This is the crunch where you have to make decisions on
what takes priority with you. The self-discipline approach explained in Chapter Eleven will be helpful. The following adapta-
tion of Scott's (1980, pp. 77-81) exercise is useful in setting
objectives when you do not know what you want.

1. Take a "wants" inventory:
    a. What I want more of is. . . .
    b. What I want less of is. . . .
2. What do you want to accomplish in your lifetime?
3. What do you want your long-term life-style to be?
4. Clarify short-term objectives:
    a. What do you want in your work life five years from
       now?
       —What do you want your job title to be?
       —Where do you want to be working?
       —What do you want your annual salary to be?
       —What associations do you want to belong to?
       —What awards do you want to earn?
    b. What do you want your personal life to be like five
       years from now?
       —What do you want in terms of family and friends?
       —Where do you want to be living?
       —What do you want to look like?
       —What skills and educational accomplishments do you
         want to have?
       —What do you want your net worth to be?
    c. What do you want in your work life one year from
       now? (Consider each question under a.)
    d. What do you want your personal life to be like one
       year from now? (Consider each question under b.)
    e. How well do your one-year objectives relate to your
       five-year objectives?

One other area that we have found to need attention is
anxiety and worry. Worry is primarily a mental and emotional

preoccupation with possible negative events in the future. The more you work on your identity and self-worth, the more self-confident you will be about handling whatever the future offers. This is easier said than done. Some ways to relieve worry are: (1) Develop a healthy attitude about time—live in the present. (2) Take your time; hurry is not necessary. (3) If you have a problem, think it through, ask for help, make a decision. (4) Be more active: run, dance, do yoga, hike. (5) If you have many things to do, make a list and set priorities. On some things, ask yourself: "What is the worst thing that would happen if I did not do this?" (6) Tackle one task at a time and finish it or take it as far as you can and let go. (7) Stop trying to be superman or superwoman. (8) Accept life's uncertainties—especially things over which you have no control. We can only do our best and then let go; of course, we are always responsible for doing the very best we can (Bloomfield and Kory, 1978).

Organizational Stress Management

There is much that organizations can do to reduce negative stress and help individuals cope with the stress of their jobs. This can start with the personnel function, ensuring that people are placed in positions that they are capable of handling and whose standards they are able to or can be trained to meet. There should be ongoing, objective-oriented training for people at all levels in the organization, including optional training in stress management. Policies supporting job rotation and cross-training so that people are not limited to one small phase of their functional area are also helpful. Managers should be held accountable for development of their employees through clarity about job and role; giving feedback, both positive and negative, on an ongoing basis; delegating with controls, giving employees the maximum appropriate freedom and control over their jobs; constantly training people and expecting improvement each year; and counseling them on their careers.

Management can support the development by managers and employees of their own stress-management programs by

providing training to increase their awareness of stress and ways
they can manage it; by establishing physical exercise programs;
by emphasizing nutrition in the cafeteria and vending machines
by providing food and snack alternatives; and by providing employee assistance programs where counseling is available to trou-
bled employees. Many hospitalization plans now provide for
payment of a large portion of therapy costs. A quiet room
could be provided for workers to use at break time as an alternative to the coffee break. In large companies where managers
are often transferred, supportive sessions could be scheduled to
help families handle the grief of breaking relationships in one
town and making new relationships in another. Quite often we
have found that when an individual's productivity declines,
there are problems at home.

Resources

In developing your own program, it is important that you
take responsibility for your health, using health professionals
and other resources as appropriate, and that you move one step
at a time, establishing priorities for what you are going to work
on first. It is very helpful to enlist the support of family members and friends. Recognize and accept that plateaus occur and
that they are only temporary—stay on your program! Meditating twice daily can be the most important discipline in helping
to keep you focused and giving you the energy—and will—to
continue.

The resources available for developing a stress-management program are abundant. The works cited in this chapter are
books we have found to be particularly helpful. Other informa-
tive sources include Adams (1980), Allen and Linde (1981),
Benson (1975), Clark (1965), Cooper (1977), Davis, Eshelman,
and McKay (1980), Frendenberger (1980), Goldberg (1978),
Goldwag (1979), McLean (1979), Selye (1974), and Ulene
(1977). Reading publications such as *New Age, East-West Journal, Prevention,* and *Medical Self-Care* will bring you in contact
with additional resources that you may wish to use. Find friends

who have goals similar to yours and share resources, experiences, and life itself. Each of us has to develop our own program for meeting our individual needs. We need to be comfortable with it and enjoy it. Remember: Try new things for at least thirty days before evaluating.

❧❧ 13 ❧❧

Techniques
for Producing
Positive Personal
Change

❧❧ ❧❧ ❧❧ ❧❧ ❧❧ ❧❧ ❧❧ ❧❧

Affirmations, visualization, and meditation are tools to help
managers use their inner resources to the fullest potential. These
are ways to tap into your spiritual dimension and produce positive results that you cannot always explain. Your spirituality is
the part of your being that is often ignored, because it cannot
always be explained logically or scientifically. If you are using
only your physical and mental parts, you are not drawing on
your full resources. These tools are helpful in calming your
mind and body, relieving stress, improving your concentration,
increasing your energy, listening to your intuition, and programming yourself to accomplish desired goals. When you are using
your internal resources fully, you become aware of the enor-
mous power that you possess to make things happen and
change yourself.

We will give an overview of these techniques, with references for exploring them in greater depth. We would like you to
"taste" these ideas and suggestions and swallow those that fit
for you. To effectively evaluate these tools, we recommend
practicing them for a minimum of thirty days before evaluating

how they are working for you. None of these concepts is new. They have been around for hundreds of years, but only recently have they received widespread attention and been used in many personal- and management-development workshops.

Relaxation and Centering

To effectively use affirmations, visualization, and meditation, you must first achieve a relaxed state. It is important that your mind is calm and not cluttered with thoughts. When you do a relaxation exercise, you become aware of the multitude of thoughts that flow through your mind, much of the time, making it difficult to concentrate on one subject or activity. When you are relaxed and centered, you are able to use affirmation and visualization techniques to program yourself to accomplish desired goals and to use meditation effectively.

When your body and mind are deeply relaxed, your brain-wave patterns actually change and become slower. This deeper, slower level is called the alpha level. It is contrasted with the beta level, the state of being fully awake and conscious; the theta level, the state of dreaming; and the delta level, the state of deep sleep. You are fully aware in the alpha state. The alpha level has been found to be far more effective than the more active beta level for creating real changes in the so-called objective world through the use of affirmations and visualization. This means that you are able to make more effective changes in your work and your life when you are in a relaxed state (Gawain, 1978).

Learning to keep yourself centered enables you to maintain a feeling of balance, a feeling of more strength, a solid integration of mind and body. In *The Centering Book* (Hendricks and Wills, 1975), children describe this centering experience as being lined up right, feeling solid, not thinking but just feeling, being "right on," and being balanced. Many teachers use these centering techniques to calm students and get them in a centered state for taking tests. The same works for adults getting ready for a difficult problem-solving meeting. When in a centered state, you are more in control of yourself and have self-assurance that all your skills and competencies are available to you when you need them. Thus, you perform at your full potential or close to it. A simple centering exercise (Hendricks and Wills, 1975) is presented here:

Find a comfortable position for yourself: sitting upright in a (straight) chair, sitting cross-legged on the floor, or lying on the floor.

Instructions (to be read to others or recorded for yourself):

"Close your eyes and let your [body] relax. Shift around a little until you find a spot where your body rests comfortably. Let a few soothing breaths flow into your body and let yourself go."

Pause (thirty seconds).

"Now feel a little spot of energy at the bottom of your stomach, in the center of your body. You may imagine it as a light, or a warm spot, or just a spot of energy. Relax your body and feel the spot of energy in the center of your body, deep within you."

Pause (fifteen seconds).

"Breathe in slowly through your nose, and, as you do, let each breath make your spot of energy larger. Breathing in on this spot makes it grow. Relax, and breathe smoothly, letting each breath make the spot a little larger. Let it expand to fill your stomach, breathing slowly and deeply."

Pause (one minute).

"Now your stomach is filled, and you may continue breathing on your stomach full of energy as it slowly expands upward to fill your chest."

Pause (one minute).

"Now feel your stomach and chest filled with energy, and, as you breathe, feel your energy expand. Now let the energy flow up through your neck into your head. Breathe slowly, and feel each breath expanding the energy into your head."

Pause (one minute).

"Let the energy circulate freely from the bottom of your stomach, up through your chest, up to the top of your head. Relax, and feel the energy flow throughout your body, and, as you do, feel those parts of your body as one. Feel the flow of energy circulate through your body."

Pause (one minute).

"Now it's time to become alert again. Begin to move your fingers and toes a little. Let your legs feel lively and full of energy. Let your eyes open slowly. When your eyes are fully open, stand up. Feel refreshed and relaxed."

There are many techniques for relaxing and getting centered. In addition to *The Centering Book*, there are *The Second Centering Book* (Hendricks and Roberts, 1977) and *The Relaxation Response* (Benson, 1975). Choose one technique or a combination of several that are comfortable for you, use it for thirty days, and then evaluate. In the beginning, we have found it helpful to put the exercise on a cassette tape and play it while you are in a relaxed position. After several times, you probably will not need the tape. In recording, read the instructions slowly, giving yourself ample time to follow them.

Grounding is a technique that can be used to keep your centeredness. It is better done when standing but can be done sitting. Get in a comfortable position and imagine that you are a tree with roots going deep into the earth below your feet. You can imagine your arms as branches of the tree that are solidly connected to the earth, as is the tree. You can then imagine the energy flowing from the tips of your branches down to your roots in the earth. You can do this whenever you wish to feel solid and connected. Sometimes in meetings, we lose our concentration and our trend of thought. When we do this, we have lost our grounding. Quickly changing to an upright sitting posture with feet flat on the floor and imagining that we are connected to the earth will help us regain our grounding, concentration, and thought processes in the here and now. The more often you do this, the faster you will be able to accomplish it in meetings or other places. Another grounding technique is imagining a rope coming from the center of the earth, up through your feet and legs, into your body, with the energy from the center of the earth flowing up through the rope and into your body. This is a way of replenishing energy when you are tired or sluggish.

Affirmations

The word *affirm* means "make firm." An affirmation is a strong, positive statement that something is already so, making firm what you are imagining (Gawain, 1978). When you experience a relaxation exercise or meditation, you become aware of the activity of your thoughts. Sometimes it is fun to let these thoughts just pass through and count them. Unfortunately, these thought forms are often negative and will color what you do. It has been said that you are what you think. If you think the worst, that is usually what will happen. We can conclude from this that we have good skills in talking to ourselves and programming ourselves to carry out our thoughts. The use of affirmations, or declarations, as they are sometimes called, allows you to replace these negative or less helpful thoughts with positive ideas that will lead you to your goals or the conditions that you want in your work and your life. It is a powerful technique that will in a short time transform your attitudes and expectations about life and thereby change what you create for yourself.

Spice (1982) teaches the use of affirmations under the title "Up Your Thinking." She advises replacing negative thoughts with positive ones: "I can't" is replaced with "I did," "that's impossible" with "that wasn't so hard," and "nothing will work" with "I can." One method of replacing thoughts is to identify existing thoughts and replace the ones that will not support performance goals with those that will. When people are fuzzy about what they want to do, have them recite out loud, "I know exactly what I want to do." For improving time management, we suggest that you think "I have all the time in the world to do what I need or want to do." With conscious selection of more useful thoughts supporting what you want to do in your professional and personal life, you become your own reinforcer. Spice comments, "Our context is 'merely' that the thoughts we have effect the reality we experience, and that we must seek harmony between stated performance goals and previously unarticulated self-perceptions. The one formula is a simple one: knowledge plus congruent beliefs equals action. Knowledge plus negating beliefs equals good intentions and often guilt" (Spice, 1982, p. 57).

Writing Affirmations. Use the present tense, not the past or the future. For example, "I organize my time each day," not "I will organize" or "I plan to organize." Be positive. Affirm the attitude you wish to have. For example, "I am relaxed at work," instead of "I don't lose my temper." Be personal. Use "I" and follow it with your name. For example, "I, Jane Doe, am solving problems creatively."

Use terms of accomplishment. State that your goal has already been achieved. For example, "My work is well organized each day," not "I am getting better organized." Be accurate and realistic. If you desire a certain weight, state that weight, not an approximate weight or one lower than desired. For example, "I weigh 155 pounds." Add drama and excitement. "I weigh 155 pounds and feel slim and trim," or "I, Joe Dokes, lead an exciting life." Use active verbs, such as "I remember names very easily" rather than "I am able to remember names."

Be positive, without comparisons. Rather than "I am getting better in listening," say "I enjoy listening to others." Avoid comparing yourself with others by using words such as *most* or *better than.* Affirm yourself only. Use "I enjoy building positive working relationships with others," rather than "My associates like me."

Using Affirmations. We recommend writing each affirmation twenty times each day for at least ten days. In this way, you are reaching your senses. You see the affirmation, and you hear it when you repeat it silently or—preferably—out loud as you write. You hear the pen scratching the paper, you feel the pen in your hand, and you touch the paper. Typing is faster for some people. It will accomplish the same result.

Each day, as you write the affirmation twenty times, be aware of any negative thoughts or feelings or barriers to achievement. Make note of these negatives and replace them with affirmations. An example of such a switch would be to change "This is boring" to a positive affirmation like "This is fun." This process is described in some detail in *The Only Diet There Is* (Ray, 1981). This delightful book has many useful affirmations and techniques for weight reduction that can be adapted to any goal you may have.

We find that working with affirmations daily, both writing them and repeating them in a relaxed state of mind, will gradually cause them to become totally integrated with your consciousness. You will notice when your mind is responding positively and you are beginning to experience the intended results. Then you can reduce the number of times you write or repeat the specific affirmations. You will find that repeating the affirmation once a day, or whenever you find yourself behaving in an undesired manner, is a good reinforcer. Once you are programmed with the positive thought, the affirmation will serve as an anchor that you can use at any time.

In addition to writing them down on paper, say them to yourself while in a relaxed state. It is easier and more effective to program your unconscious while in this alpha state. The positive statement becomes a part of you, and you will find yourself unconsciously doing what you wish to do. We also recommend that you put your affirmation on cards. Display them in prominent places (bedroom mirror, bathroom, desk at office and home, sun visor of car, wallet, dining room table, and so forth) to constantly remind you. Repeating the affirmation while stopped in traffic is a productive use of this time.

The time that it takes to reprogram yourself will vary according to how deep-seated your old behavior is. A friend of ours required many months to achieve forgiveness through affirmations and visualization. Now a recitation of his forgiveness affirmation will quickly remove hostile thoughts of retribution and blaming from his conscious mind. Visualizing the end result while saying the affirmation strengthens the programming and will speed up the process. Another reinforcement is putting your affirmations on a cassette tape and listening to them each day. The only limit to the number of affirmations that you can work with at the same time is the amount of time you make available for this powerful effort.

Some examples of affirmations that you can use in the area of managing are "I delegate to my subordinates with clarity," "All my projects are profitable," "I identify problems in order to gain successful solutions," "I make good decisions when I have the facts," and "I put others at ease with my sincerity." For increasing self-worth, you might use "My skills and special experience attract special opportunities," "Positive thoughts bring benefits I desire," "I have the right to feel good about myself," "My body is now free of any tension, and I feel good everywhere," "I am whole and complete within myself," or "I deserve to get compliments on my accomplishments." If you wish to achieve greater calmness, you could use affirmations such as "I am completely calm when people disagree with me," "People can reject my ideas without rejecting me," "I no longer resent John Smith and forgive him completely," "I have the right to say no to people without losing their friendship," and "Other people have the right to say no to me without hurting me." And examples of affirmations useful in the area of success are "I am always in the right place at the right time, successfully engaged in the right activity," "I now have enough time, energy, wisdom, and money to accomplish all my desires," "Money flows to me freely and effortlessly," "My ability to complete transactions compliments my skill at finding good deals," and "I deserve the very best in life."

As you can see, there is no limit to how affirmations can be used—in fact, you can use an affirmation to start this process: "Every day, I write my affirmations twenty times." It takes practice and repetition. Do it for thirty days and then evaluate. You will probably be pleasantly surprised with the results.

Visualization

Visualization is the process by which an individual mentally pictures a desired goal or result, creating his or her own positive models in the mind. In setting objectives, we have found it helpful to visualize the end result before writing the objective. This makes it easier to avoid the activity trap. When we think in terms of the end result, it is easier to see the alternative paths available to accomplish the objective.

Visualization techniques are being used widely in athletics and cancer treatment. *Getting Well Again* (Simonton, Matthews-Simonton, and Creighton, 1978) describes the visualization and imagery work being used with cancer patients with some interesting results. Russell (Russell and Branch, 1979) of the Boston Celtics describes how he found that when he visualized new plays and moves on the back of his eyelids after watching other stars perform, he could execute these moves on the basketball court. Garfield (1982) describes how athletes and business executives use these techniques to improve their performance. In his research with "terminally ill" patients who recovered, he found that they felt they used hidden reserves that they had been unaware of. In his seminars on peak performance, Garfield trains people to visualize themselves performing successfully. "To use this master skill, you have to learn to relax enough to plant images of excellent performance. Whether it's in a sport or on a job, you'll begin to perform that way. You mentally rehearse. Peak performers view their imaginations as internal playing grounds; they have learned to control the images they send to their brains" (Garfield, 1982, p. 6).

Successful visualization relies on this most basic type of learning—the creation and patterning of ourselves after the perfect and rich images we envision. Henry Kaiser conceded that every one of his business accomplishments was realized first in his imagination, long before he achieved it in the real world. Conrad Hilton, too, said that he visualized himself running a hotel many years before he purchased his first one (McKay, Davis, and Fannig, 1981). Emil Coué, a French pharmacist, believed that you can persuade yourself through your imagination to do anything that is physically possible. Belief in success inspires success. Coué argued that our thoughts, good or bad, become concrete reality. He was convinced that physical diseases are generally more easily cured than mental ones (Trubo, 1982).

By forming an image, you can make a clear mental statement of what you want to accomplish. By repeating this image

again and again, you come to expect that what you want will
occur. In addition to consciously programming change through
these positive images, you can use visualization to gain access
to your unconscious mind. The potency of imagery can be
found in the research of physiologist Edmund Jacobson, who
has shown that when an individual visually imagines running,
there are small but measurable contractions in the muscles,
comparable to the changes that occur during actual running.
Similarly, by holding the image of being chased by a vicious
mad dog, you can raise your blood pressure, accelerate your
pulse rate, and even provoke goosebumps and perspiration.
Steve DeVore, an educational psychologist and a specialist in
visualization, states that if you can get in touch with the sounds
associated with your objectives as well as the tastes and odor,
you have taken a great step forward toward achieving your goal.
What you are doing is flooding the brain and nervous system
with pure, specific, sensory vision of what you desire. Electro-
chemistry has shown us that the brain incorporates all these details as if they were already accomplished.

Developing Visualization Skills. To use visualization, it is
not necessary to "see" an image. Some people are able to see
clear, sharp images with their eyes closed; others state that they
do not actually see anything but just "think about" it or
imagine that they are looking at it. Since you use your imagination regularly, continue with whatever approach you find yourself using. The following exercise, adapted from *Creative Visualization* (Gawain, 1978, pp. 13-14) will help you to understand
what it means to visualize:

> Close your eyes and relax deeply (this may
> require five minutes using an exercise you are com-
> fortable with). Think of a room that is familiar to
> you. Remember the details of the room, color of
> the carpet, pieces of furniture, where they are lo-
> cated, windows, pictures, etc. Imagine yourself
> walking into the room and sitting in one of the
> chairs.
>
> Now with your eyes still closed, visualize a
> pleasant experience (situation) you have had in re-

cent weeks. Remember the experience as vividly and in as much detail as possible. Enjoy, again, the pleasurable sensations you had at that time.

Now imagine that you are in a setting from nature—grass, stream, woods, and so on—and put yourself in this scene. It may be a place you have been or a picture you have seen. Think of the details and create it the way you would like it to be.

Practicing an exercise similar to this daily will improve your visualization skills until you can visualize your goals. Visualizing a goal is more important than knowing every detail of how you will reach it. When you set out to climb a mountain, you need a clear image of the top of the hill. You do not need to know every twist or turn of the trail or the functions of your muscles. Gawain (1978) identifies four basic steps for creative visualization: (1) setting your goal; (2) creating a clear idea or picture; (3) focusing on it often; and (4) giving it positive energy with strong affirmations and feelings that the goal is real and possible.

Using Visualization. Visualization and imagery are even more effective when used with affirmations in a relaxed state of mind. There are three elements in you that influence your success—desire, belief, and acceptance. You must have a clear, strong feeling of purpose—something you really want or desire. The more you believe in a chosen goal and the possibility of attaining it, the more likely it is that you will attain it. You must be willing to accept and have what you are seeking! We have found that people often set and work toward goals that they think they should not and do not really want to achieve. Using this visualization technique will make you aware of whether these are the goals you really want in your life. If you discover that these goals are not what you want, it is appropriate for you to use life and career planning to clarify your situation.

Meditation

Meditation is a process, not a state. It is a continuous stream of effortless concentration over an extended period of time. LeShan (1974) describes it as being like coming home. A goal of meditation is the fullest use of what it means to be human. The attainment of the meditative state is another way of perceiving and relating to reality while achieving a greater efficiency and enthusiasm for everyday life.

Neurenberger (1981) points out that *meditation* is not a religious word, although it is used in many religions. He calls it a practical, systematic method that allows one (1) to understand oneself at all levels of being, (2) to understand one's environment completely, (3) to eliminate and prevent inner conflicts, and (4) to obtain a tranquil and peaceful mind. It is a personal technique for increasing internal awareness and expanding conscious self-control. It is a tool, not a way of life.

Meditation is practiced extensively in Eastern cultures, and many of the teachers of meditation are Indian yogis and Buddhist monks who meditate long periods each day. These people are noted for their relaxed warmth, openness, and alertness, no matter what the situation. Some highly pressured members of organizations in our busy society resist taking the time to relax. When Benson (1974) wrote an article in the *Harvard Business Review* urging businesses to give employees time for a meditation break, there was a flood of letters protesting that stress and tension were essential to good business management and suggesting that meditation would make zombies of us. It is interesting that Harry Truman and Winston Churchill were but two of many world leaders who used brief rest periods of this sort to sustain their energy and vitality. It has been said that fifteen to twenty minutes of meditation is comparable to two hours of sleep. We have found that if we are tired before starting a trip, the most relaxing thing we can do is to meditate for fifteen minutes with a focus on a safe arrival at the destination. We are then refreshed, with sufficient energy for the trip. The positive payoff, organizationally and individually, will be discussed in the following paragraphs.

Benefits of Meditation. In *The Holistic Way to Health and Happiness,* Bloomfield and Kory (1978, pp. 64-65) presented a list they had compiled from a review of more than 400 published scientific studies on the results of meditation. Their list includes the following beneficial effects:

Effects on physical health:

1. Increased energy.
2. Increased resistance to disease.
3. Increased physical capacity to handle stress.
4. Improved mind-body coordination and physical agility.
5. Reduced incidence of insomnia, tension headaches, and bodily aches and pains.
6. Control of high blood pressure.
7. Relief of psychosomatic conditions such as asthma, neuro-dermatitis, and gastrointestinal problems.
8. Help in normalizing weight.

Effects on mental and emotional well-being:

9. Reduced anxiety and nervousness.
10. Reduced depression.
11. Reduced neuroticism and inhibitions.
12. Reduced irritability.
13. Improved self-esteem and self-regard.
14. Increased ego strength.
15. Improved problem-solving ability.
16. Improved organization of thinking.
17. Increased creativity.
18. Increased productivity.

Effects on spiritual well-being:

19. Promotion of self-actualization.
20. Fostering of trust, capacity for intimate contact.
21. Enhanced ability to love and express affection.
22. Development of inner wholeness.
23. Increased autonomy and self-reliance.
24. Increased satisfaction at home and at work.
25. Reduced feelings of alienation and meaninglessness.
26. Strengthening of religious affiliations.

Our experience with meditation substantiates many of these findings. At the office, when we are feeling low on energy in midafternoon or have many things to do and feel fragmented, fifteen minutes of relaxation and meditation gives us sufficient energy to complete the tasks before us, as well as a sense of direction. At home, meditation after morning exercise gives us energy, calmness, and guidance for the day and helps us to feel more enthusiastic and positive about what the day has to offer. An evening meditation, before sleep or before dinner, also is helpful in achieving calmness and direction. The before-dinner meditation usually results in a decreased desire for alcohol and food, supporting our weight goal. The before-sleep meditation results in more restful sleep and pleasant dreams.

Meditative Techniques. There are many theories on the proper way to meditate. We think that the best way is the one that is most comfortable and effective for you. This may be a combination of several techniques. However, there are some basic factors to be considered. Muktananda (1980) describes four factors in meditation. The first is dealing with the mind. We cannot subdue our mind forcibly and should avoid focusing on any one thought. It is advisable to let your thoughts pass through and let the mind wander wherever it likes. Gradually, your mind will become calm; that is meditation. The second factor is using a mantra, which is a Sanskrit term for a word or phrase that is repeated continuously. This repeated recitation is an effective technique of disengaging the mind. Muktananda's mantra is "Om Namah Shivaya" ("I bow to the Lord"). Other simple mantras are "I am" and "Let go." The third factor is the posture that you take when meditating. This may be sitting in a chair, sitting on the floor in a "lotus" position (legs folded one over the other), or lying with your back flat on the floor. It is important that the spine be straight. The position you use should be one that you can stay in comfortably, without moving, for the duration of your meditation, although some individuals say that such activities as walking, running, music, prayer, and looking at a mandala can also be used as a form of meditation. In other words, any activity you invest with prolonged and focused attention can be a form of meditation. The fourth factor described by Muktananda is the breathing process. Breathing should be natural and spontaneous. We should not disturb the natural rhythm of the breath, which works in conjunction with the mind. Focusing on your breathing may be all that you need to get into a meditative state. If a mantra is used, it should be synchronized with your breathing.

In preparation for meditation, it is well to select a quiet place where you will not be disturbed. It is desirable to use the same place each day if possible. It is also recommended that you meditate at the same time each day for a minimum of fifteen minutes each time. Three times a day is optimum. We find that when we meditate for three fifteen-minute periods a day, we achieve many of the effects described earlier. When not meditating, we are not as effective in our work and other activities.

To develop your own meditative style, we recommend reading some of the books on meditation, taking training from an experienced meditator, or getting some tapes for guided meditations. You may wish to make your own tapes to help you get started. A support group is also helpful here. The important consideration is to do it and have patience. Do not punish yourself if your thoughts drift off or you doze. Gently bring yourself back to your breathing or mantra. There will be dry periods and plateaus where you think nothing is happening. Keep on meditating and remember that there is no one right way.

Relaxation, affirmations, visualization, and meditation can be integrated and used together for positive results. When you are in the relaxed meditative state (alpha state), it is much easier to program your unconscious to accomplish the goals you want and manage the stress in your life. These powerful tools will help you achieve a positive attitude and a positive environment of hope and achievement.

⚡ Conclusion ⚡

Implementing
Positive Practices:
A Plan for Action

After deciding to implement the positive practices presented in this book, a manager has to decide where to start: with the organization, with individuals and teams, or with him- or herself. We recommend an organized approach, starting with a diagnosis of the organization, the team, and the self. Then the manager can identify the barriers to successful implementation, set objectives, and determine what resources will be needed. This chapter will provide direction for taking these steps and will present some of the potential payoffs for the manager using positive practices.

Diagnosis

The first step will start with a self-diagnosis by the manager to determine his or her leadership style, success with that style, and satisfaction or dissatisfaction with the results that it is producing in the organization. This may lead to the discovery that there is a difference between how the manager perceives his or her management style and how it is perceived by subordinates. Self-diagnosis may be made with the help of a consultant or associates in the organization. With the information it produces, the manager can proceed to choose which positive practices to add to his or her managerial behavior.

The second area of diagnosis involves both the manager and the work team. The group can look at the way they are working as a team and decide what they would like to change and which positive practices help them achieve the change. This approach has a better chance of success than implementation of these concepts by the manager alone, because the team members can act as a support group, giving feedback to the manager and each other.

The third step is the organizational diagnosis, which is necessary if positive practices are to be implemented in a total organizational approach. This diagnosis can use formal surveys to determine the attitudes, values, norms, and needs of managers and employees, providing factual data on the organization and how it is being managed. Managers throughout the organization can share the results with their subordinates and work with them to determine what they want to change and what they need to do to accomplish the change. Some of these surveys will identify the gap between what is and what the people in the organization would like.

The next step is for the manager and team to develop a description of what the organization will be like and what they will be doing when it is being managed in the manner desired. Then they can decide how these positive practices can help them accomplish the desired outcome. Once this outcome is clear, goals and objectives can be established and a detailed plan of action developed. This plan should include the known obstacles and strategies to overcome them, the resources necessary to achieve the goal, and a clear program for regularly evaluating progress. A time schedule and responsibility chart are necessary so that accountability and support can be managed. The action plan will make it possible to determine the consulting and training resources that will be needed to facilitate the change process. These are usually a combination of external and internal resources, depending on the training capabilities within the organization. It is essential that management be committed to this action plan and prepared to continue with it for a long time, despite inevitable setbacks and failures.

Such long-term consistency and stability can be seen in five teams in the National Football League—the Dallas Cowboys, the Los Angeles Raiders, the Miami Dolphins, the Pittsburgh Steelers, and the Minnesota Vikings. These teams have represented their conferences in the majority of the Superbowls and seldom have a losing season. John Madden of the Raiders has remarked that developing a team personality takes time and that it involves not just coaching but the whole organization. The teams mentioned here have had the same owners and substantially the same management for years. Tex Schramm of the Dallas Cowboys remarked that when you have a problem, you do not change the people, you attack the problem. Having patience to work out problems is important. We think that the philosophy of these successful football teams is applicable in most organizations.

Where to Start

For a total organization change, the process must start with the chief executive officer and the management team and gradually move downward through the organization. Managers must not only announce the changes that they want but also model the new behavior themselves. As mentioned in the Introduction to this book, this is the optimal place to start to assure support for the change on a continuing basis.

The next best place to start is with the manager of a semi-autonomous unit—a region or district, a plant, or a function, such as the data-processing unit. The chance of success in these cases is usually better when the unit is geographically separate from the central office and the unit manager has the support of a higher-level manager who will tolerate a possible decline in productivity in the short range in return for solid growth in the long range. Such support is not essential, but the risk of failure is much greater without it. One manager of a regional office who chose to use positive practices in his region without the support of his superior in the central office achieved considerable success, including moving from low producer to one of the top performers in the system. The main office recognized his achievement by assigning his personnel special projects. His region also produced more promotable managers. Both he and his assistant were promoted to top positions in the central office.

The third place to start is with the individual managers. They can use many of these positive practices in their own development and the development of the members of their teams. We recommend strongly that managers be able to call on support people who have the same goals or who at least understand and support the behavior change desired. Managers should let their higher-level managers know what they are doing whether or not they have their managers' support. They should move slowly and avoid making too many changes in their management style too rapidly. In any event, they must maintain performance and profitability to keep their higher-level managers happy. We feel that the use of positive practices by any manager will ultimately pay off in higher productivity and better decision making.

Eliminating Barriers to Change

The barriers to the use of positive practices may come from within the manager, within the members of the team, or within the organization culture, values, and norms. Among the barriers to using positive practices are low self-worth, fear, and resistance to change. These are often caused by a negative culture, a closed system, or an activity orientation. It is necessary to identify these barriers in each system and work deliberately to change them to be supportive of positive practices. If this is not done, the change effort will be sabotaged intentionally or unintentionally, and the organization will continue to operate as it has in the past.

We have found that the low self-worth of managers is a primary obstacle. When they have low self-worth, managers will be insecure, will fear change, and will hang onto the past, preserving the status quo at all cost. This is a highly dependent position of waiting for someone else to take action, with a norm of avoiding problem solving and conflict. The energy depleters (hopelessness, helplessness, and powerlessness) are fully operational. In their resistance to change, managers will not see the choices and opportunities available to them and will tend to be defensive when confronted or given innovative suggestions for change. With these negative feelings about self, managers usually have negative feelings about others. This results in policing and overcontrol of people, which stifle creativity and innovation. People are treated as things, or pieces of furniture, instead of human beings. In this environment, there is considerable blaming and criticism, destructive confrontation or avoidance of confrontation, threats of punishment, and low utilization of human resources. Technical and material resources are considered more important than human resources, even though management may say that human resources are most important.

The insecurity of managers often stems from fear of the unknown and discomfort with ambiguity. This leads to a lack of flexibility and many rigid rules and regulations. Preserving the system tends to be more important than serving the customer and getting the job done. There is an unwillingness to take risks; when decisions have to be made, the data will be analyzed, debated, and reworked for fear of making a mistake or hope that the problem will go away without the necessity of risking a decision. As a result of this insecurity, managers may avoid talking with their subordinates, peers, and superiors or fail to clarify mutual expectations and standards of satisfactory performance. These poor communications result in inadequate accountability and support, with performance evaluation feedback (positive and negative), and confrontation either avoided or done poorly or destructively. When this condition exists, substandard performance is condoned. In some cases, substandard employees have been allowed to remain in this state for years or have even been promoted, to transfer the problem to someone else. This environment contributes to labor problems, since management and employees are not communicating straight with each other.

Individual barriers may be supported and perpetuated by

organization norms and values, either explicit or implicit. For example, an activity orientation, instead of an organization-results orientation, supports an emphasis on individual functions: managers think only of their unit or themselves and are not committed to the success of the whole organization. When this condition exists, there is considerable blaming and little cooperation. Much energy is put into protecting oneself and one's turf rather than finding ways to work with others to solve problems and to improve and innovate for the good of the organization. This leads to gaps in performance and overlap of duties. Organizationally, this supports a closed-system environment, blocking information and help from external sources. Some of the cultural norms that may affect the implementation of positive practices are rewards, communications, resource allocation, confrontation, training, orientation, and modeled behavior.

To remove or lessen barriers to change, the manager and team will have to set objectives and allocate the necessary resources. These may include individual-development training and group training in the areas that are blocking the use of positive practices. The manager should initiate training. In large organizations, the training department must be responsive to the manager's needs and be held accountable for achieving the training objectives that support the desired behavior change on the job. In smaller organizations, external resources can be recruited to fulfill the training needs. External seminars and workshops may be used to supplement internal training as individual needs are identified. Some managers have used external training to develop their skills and then successfully used these skills in internal training.

Managers also need feedback systems to help them establish positive practices. Feedback is especially important when a manager's behavior contradicts the positive practices he or she espouses. Feedback can come from peers, superiors, team members, consultants, or a combination of these sources. As pointed out often, a support system is essential during implementation of this change process.

This book can be used as an ongoing reference by the

manager and team to check on their progress and the next steps to be taken. Establishing, maintaining, and renewing positive practices is a never-ending effort, as it is easy to slip back into old behavior, especially in times of crisis or emergency.

Results of Positive Practices

In deciding whether to use positive practices, managers should consider the potential results, both personal and organizational. One of the outcomes should be the satisfaction of both organizational and personal needs through the management process. We find that the use of positive practices is a developmental experience for the individual manager, the team, and the organization. When people know how they are contributing to organization results and participate in decisions that affect them, there will be commitment, motivation, and openness to change through the norm of constant improvement of performance.

The commitment to organization results makes it necessary for managers and their employees to keep in close touch with their customers or clients, both inside and outside the organization, as they must meet the needs of these customers or clients in order to perform acceptably in their jobs and for their organization to be successful. Such commitment also requires a high level of cooperation with others, so that teamwork becomes a norm in the organization for which subordinates are held accountable and supported. With this commitment to organization results, there will be an openness to new ideas from all levels within the organization and from customers or clients and other sources outside the organization. Employees will not be satisfied with the status quo or with resting on their laurels from past performances. The system not only will be open to ideas from the outside but will deliberately seek new ideas. With this openness will come constant awareness of changes in the marketplace and in other systems that influence the success of the organization. Consequently, there will be less chance for surprises and crisis management.

Another payoff from positive practices is the positive

attitude that will exist. This attitude will start with individual self-worth, which is a basis of positive practices. When people have high self-worth, they are more aware of their own identity and take responsibility for their own behavior. They will have self-assurance and confidence in their ability to solve problems, individually and collectively. With this attitude, almost anything is possible—decisions and solutions to problems can far exceed expectations. The energy providers of hopefulness, helpfulness, and powerfulness will be fully operative. People will be open to change and aware of their choices and will take advantage of opportunities. We often see this in sports. When players have a positive attitude about themselves and their teammates and are playing as a team, they often are able to defeat teams with higher individual capabilities but negative attitudes about themselves and their teammates. With this positive attitude and receptivity to change, it is easier for managers to introduce new systems or new technology. They are able to let go of the past and live in the present, looking to the future; they are able to handle crises and sudden changes without panicking. With high self-worth and positive feelings about others, there will be little or no attacking of people's self-esteem. Confrontation will be a way of life because of the commitment to organizational success but will be focused on unsatisfactory behavior or performance rather than on the person. Every attempt will be made to ensure that the person confronted does not feel personally rejected.

Another advantage of positive practices is that they enable managers to manage accountability and support at the same time, with the realization that humanness and productivity go hand in hand and are not contradictory. Managers with high self-worth are better able to manage in a caring though tough-minded manner; they stay in close touch with their employees by circulating throughout their organization, interacting, listening, and responding as appropriate. Employees get the information and resources that they need to do their jobs effectively and thus are highly motivated to contribute to the good of the organization. They are stimulated to make suggestions and use their creative skills to improve performance and listen and respond to each other. This creates a high level of trust and good relations between managers and their subordinates, whether or not there is a union, and helps eliminate the adversary relationship that so often exists between management and employees.

With positive practices, managers will be clear with their employees about acceptable standards of job performance and work expectations. In managing accountability, they will give regular feedback on performance—both positive and negative, and as soon as possible after incidents. Evaluation will be provided on a regular basis, not limited to the once-a-year performance appraisal. This process will identify developmental needs of employees, and programs will be developed and implemented to improve their skills and knowledge. This organizational commitment to the development of human resources will result in individual motivation and commitment, which, in the long range, will improve productivity and profitability while reducing absenteeism, turnover, and health problems.

Our experience has been that the results of the use of positive practices are often very subtle. Change occurs slowly and is not immediately perceived, but when the manager and team stop to evaluate, they see how things have changed, how they are operating together better, feeling better about themselves and their associates, and achieving better organization results. Managers must be patient and not expect positive results immediately, although there might be some. The real payoff comes in the long range and will have a positive impact on the bottom line, provided that there are no obstacles beyond the control of the manager, such as adverse legislation or technological or market changes.

In summary, implementation requires identifying the desired organization results, developing a plan of action, sticking with the plan while allowing appropriate flexibility, committing resources, and evaluating regularly. The organization values articulated must be lived daily and permeate the entire organization. There must be patience, persistence, perseverance, and discipline. This is not a panacea. It requires much hard work that at times may be painful. The result is knowing that what you are doing is worth while, that you have hope, and that you are achieving things for yourselves while you are accomplishing for the organization. This all adds up to the freedom and fulfillment that come with feeling good about yourself—and that is what counts in life!

Selected Bibliography

Adams, J. D. *Understanding and Managing Stress.* San Diego, Calif.: University Associates, 1980.

Adams, J. D. (ed.). *Transforming Work.* Alexandria, Va.: Miles River Press, 1984.

Albrecht, K. *Brain Power.* Englewood Cliffs, N.J.: Prentice-Hall, 1980.

Alexander, M. "Organizational Norms Questionnaire." In J. W. Pfeiffer and J. E. Jones (eds.), *The 1978 Annual Handbook for Group Facilitators.* La Jolla, Calif.: University Associates, 1978.

Allen, R. F., and Dyer, F. J. "A Tool for Tapping the Organizational Unconscious." *Personnel Journal,* 1980, *59* (3), 192–199.

Allen, R. F., and Kraft, C. *Beat the System!* New York: McGraw-Hill, 1980.

Allen, R. F., and Kraft, C. *The Organizational Unconscious.* Englewood Cliffs, N.J.: Prentice-Hall, 1982.

Allen, R. F., and Linde, S. *Lifegain.* East Norwalk, Conn.: Appleton-Century-Crofts, 1981.

Alutto, J. A. Unpublished letter of nomination for Phillips Award, School of Management, State University of New York at Buffalo, 1978.

Beck, A. C., and Hillmar, E. D. *A Practical Approach to Organization Development Through MBO: Selected Readings.* Reading, Mass.: Addison-Wesley, 1972.

Beck, A. C., and Hillmar, E. D. *Making MBO/R Work.* Reading, Mass.: Addison-Wesley, 1976.

Beck, A. C., and Hillmar, E. D. "The Power of Positive Management." *Personnel Journal,* 1983, *62* (2), 126-131.

Beck, A. C., and Hillmar, E. D. "What Managers Can Do to Turn Around Negative Attitudes in an Organization." *Management Review,* 1984, *73* (1), 22-25.

Beckhard, R., and Harris, R. T. *Organizational Transitions: Managing Complex Change.* Reading, Mass.: Addison-Wesley, 1977.

Bell, C. "Energize Your Staff to Improve Productivity." *Management Review,* 1982, *71* (2), 46-51.

Benson, H. "Your Innate Asset for Combating Stress." *Harvard Business Review,* 1974, *52* (4), 49-60.

Benson, H. *The Relaxation Response.* New York: Avon, 1975.

Bloomfield, H. H., and Kory, R. B. *The Holistic Way to Health and Happiness.* New York: Simon & Schuster, 1978.

Bradford, D. L., and Cohen, A. R. *Managing for Excellence.* New York: Wiley, 1984a.

Bradford, D. L., and Cohen, A. R. "The Postheroic Leader." *Training and Development Journal,* 1984b, *38* (1), 40-49.

Brown, J. K. "Corporate Soul-Searching." *Across the Board,* 1984, *21* (3), 44-52.

Burns, J. M. *Leadership.* New York: Harper & Row, 1978.

Buzan, T. *Using Both Sides of Your Brain.* New York: Dutton, 1976.

Campbell, D. P. "Characteristics of Creative Managers." *Issues and Observations,* 1978, *5* (1), 6.

Clark, L. *Get Well Naturally.* New York: Arco, 1965.

Clarkson, W. M. E. "Managing for Today and Tomorrow." Address presented at Ecology of Work Conference, Pittsburgh, Pa., June 1982.

Clinebell, H. J., and Clinebell, C. N. *The Intimate Marriage.* New York: Harper & Row, 1970.

Cohen, A. R., and others. *Effective Behavior in Organizations.* Homewood, Ill.: Irwin, 1980.

Cooper, K. H. *The Aerobics Way.* New York: Bantam Books, 1977.

"Creativity." *Christopher News Notes,* Apr. 1978, no. 233.

Crockett, W. J. "The Emerging World of the Manager." *Training and Development Journal,* 1981, *35* (4), 76–85.

Davis, M., Eshelman, E., and McKay, M. *The Relaxation and Stress Reduction Workbook.* Richmond, Calif.: New Harbinger Publications, 1980.

Davis, S. M. *Managing Corporate Culture.* Cambridge, Mass.: Ballinger, 1984.

Deal, T. E., and Kennedy, A. A. *Corporate Cultures.* Reading, Mass.: Addison-Wesley, 1982.

Delbecq, A. L., Van de Ven, A. H., and Gustafson, D. H. *Group Techniques for Program Planning.* Glenview, Ill.: Scott, Foresman, 1975.

Drucker, P. F. *The Practice of Management.* New York: Harper & Row, 1954.

Drucker, P. F. *Management: Tasks, Responsibilities, Practices.* New York: Harper & Row, 1974.

Ferguson, T. "A Conversation with Ken Pelletier." *Medical Self-Care Magazine,* 1978, no. 5, 3–10.

Flowers, V. S., Hughes, C. L., Myers, M. S., and Myers, S. S. *Managerial Values for Working.* New York: AMACOM, 1975.

French, J. R. P., and Raven, B. "The Bases of Social Power." In D. Cartwright and A. Zander (eds.), *Studies in Social Power.* Ann Arbor, Mich.: Institute of Social Research, 1959.

Frendenberger, H. J. *Burn Out.* New York: Bantam Books, 1980.

Friedman, M., and Rosenman, R. H. *Type A Behavior and Your Heart.* New York: Fawcett, 1974.

Garfield, C. A. "How to Be a Peak Performer." *Bank American World,* 1982, *10* (1), 5–7.

Gawain, S. *Creative Visualization.* New York: Bantam Books, 1978.

Gilbert, T. F. *Human Competence.* New York: McGraw-Hill, 1978.

Goldberg, P. *Executive Health.* New York: McGraw-Hill, 1978.

Goldwag, E. M. (ed.). *Inner Balance.* Englewood Cliffs, N.J.: Prentice-Hall, 1979.

Greenwald, J. A. *Be the Person You Were Meant to Be.* New York: Dell, 1974.

Harrison, R. "Role Negotiation." In M. L. Berger and R. S. Berger (eds.), *Group Training Techniques.* New York: Wiley, 1974.

Hatvany, N., and Pucik, V. "Japanese Management Practices and Productivity." *Organizational Dynamics,* 1981, *9* (4), 5-21.

Hayes, J. L. "The AMA Model of Superior Performance. Part II: How Can I Do a Better Job as a Manager?" *Management Review,* 1980, *69* (2), 2-3.

Hendricks, G., and Roberts, T. B. *The Second Centering Book.* Englewood Cliffs, N.J.: Prentice-Hall, 1977.

Hendricks, G., and Wills, R. *The Centering Book.* Englewood Cliffs, N.J.: Prentice-Hall, 1975.

Herman, S. M., and Korenich, M. *Authentic Management.* Reading, Mass.: Addison-Wesley, 1977.

Herrman, N. "The Creative Brain." *Training and Development Journal,* 1981, *35* (10), 11.

Holmes, T. H., and Rahe, R. H. "The Social Readjustment Rating Scale." *Journal of Psychosomatic Research,* 1967, *2,* 213-218.

Houston, J. *The Possible Human.* Los Angeles: Tarcher, 1982.

Hughes, C. L., and Flowers, V. S. *Value Systems Analysis: Study Guide.* Dallas: Center for Values Research, 1978.

Huxley, L. A. *You Are Not the Target.* Beverly Hills, Calif.: Leighton Printing Company, 1963.

Ingalls, J. D. *Human Energy.* Reading, Mass.: Addison-Wesley, 1976.

Jones, J. E. "Role Clarification: A Team Building Activity." In J. W. Pfeiffer and J. E. Jones (eds.), *A Handbook of Structured Experiences for Human Relations Training.* Vol. 5. La Jolla, Calif.: University Associates, 1975.

Jongeward, D. *Everybody Wins: Transactional Analysis Applied to Organizations.* Reading, Mass.: Addison-Wesley, 1973.

Josefowitz, N. *Paths to Power.* Reading, Mass.: Addison-Wesley, 1980.

Kanter, R. M. *The Change Masters.* New York: Simon & Schuster, 1983.

Karp, H. B. "Team Building from a Gestalt Perspective." In J. W. Pfeiffer and J. E. Jones (eds.), *The 1980 Annual Handbook for Group Facilitators*. San Diego, Calif.: University Associates, 1980.

Kast, F. E., and Rosenzweig, J. E. *Organization and Management*. New York: McGraw-Hill, 1974.

Keirsey, D., and Bates, M. *Please Understand Me*. Del Mar, Calif.: Prometheus Nemesis Books, 1978.

Kiefer, C. F., and Senge, P. M. "Metanoic Organizations." In J. D. Adams (ed.), *Transforming Work*. Alexandria, Va.: Miles River Press, 1984.

Kiefer, C. F., and Stroh, P. "A New Paradigm for Developing Organizations." In J. D. Adams (ed.), *Transforming Work*. Alexandria, Va.: Miles River Press, 1984.

Kuhn, A., and Beam, R. D. *The Logic of Organization: A System-Based, Social Science Framework for Organization*. San Francisco: Jossey-Bass, 1982.

LeShan, L. *How to Meditate*. Boston: Little, Brown, 1974.

McClelland, D. C. *The Achieving Society*. New York: Irvington, 1961.

McClelland, D. C. *Power: The Inner Experience*. New York: Irvington, 1975.

McCoy, B. H. "Applying the Art of Action-Oriented Decision Making to the Knotty Issues of Everyday Business Life." *Management Review*, 1983, 72 (7), 20–24.

McGregor, D. *The Human Side of Enterprise*. New York: McGraw-Hill, 1960.

McKay, M., Davis, M., and Fannig, P. *Thoughts and Feelings*. Richmond, Calif.: New Harbinger Publications, 1981.

McLean, A. A. *Work Stress*. Reading, Mass.: Addison-Wesley, 1979.

Mager, R. F. *Goal Analysis*. Belmont, Calif.: Fearon, 1972.

Maidment, R. *Straight Talk*. Gretna, La.: Pelican, 1983.

Maslow, A. H. *Toward a Psychology of Being*. New York: D. Van Nostrand, 1968.

Masters, R., and Houston, J. *Mind Games*. New York: Dell, 1972.

May, R. *Courage to Create*. New York: Norton, 1975.

Miller, D. B. *Personal Vitality.* Reading, Mass.: Addison-Wesley, 1977.

Miller, E. C. " 'Hire in Haste, Repent at Leisure': The Team Selection Process at Graphic Controls." *Organizational Dynamics,* 1980, *8* (4), 3–26.

Morrison, J. H., and O'Hearne, J. J. *Practical Transactional Analysis in Management.* Reading, Mass.: Addison-Wesley, 1977.

Muktananda, S. *Meditate.* Albany: State University of New York Press, 1980.

Murphy, M. H., and White, R. A. *The Psychic Side of Sports.* Reading, Mass.: Addison-Wesley, 1978.

Myers, I. B., and Myers, P. B. *Gifts Differing.* Palo Alto, Calif.: Consulting Psychologists Press, 1980.

Naisbitt, J. *Megatrends.* New York: Warner Books, 1982.

Nash, M. *Managing Organizational Performance.* San Francisco: Jossey-Bass, 1983.

Nelson, L., and Burns, F. L. "High Performance Programming: A Framework for Transforming Organizations." In J. D. Adams (ed.), *Transforming Work.* Alexandria, Va.: Miles River Press, 1984.

Neurenberger, P. *Freedom from Stress.* Honesdale, Pa.: Himalayan International Institute of Yoga, Science and Philosophy, 1981.

Odiorne, G. A. "Scenario Writing Is a Very Useful Tool for Setting Nonquantitative Objectives." *George Odiorne Letter,* 1978, *8* (11), 1–2.

Odiorne, G. A. "Ask George Odiorne." *George Odiorne Letter,* 1984, *14* (3), 4.

Osborn, R. N., Hunt, J. G., and Jauch, L. R. *Organization Theory: An Integrated Approach.* New York: Wiley, 1980.

Osborne, C. G. *The Art of Learning to Love Yourself.* Grand Rapids, Mich.: Zondervan, 1976.

Oshry, B. "Power and Powerlessness: Good and Lousy Gardening." *Social Change,* 1976, *6* (4), 3–6, 8.

Pareek, V. "Interrole Exploration." In J. W. Pfeiffer and J. E. Jones (eds.), *The 1976 Annual Handbook for Group Facilitators.* La Jolla, Calif.: University Associates, 1976.

Parnes, S. J. *The Magic of Your Mind.* Buffalo, N.Y.: Creative Education Foundation, 1981.

Pascale, R. T., and Athos, A. G. *The Art of Japanese Management.* New York: Simon & Schuster, 1981.

Peck, M. S. *The Road Less Traveled.* New York: Simon & Schuster, 1978.

Perham, J. "The Antisocial Executive." *Dun's Business Month,* 1983, *122* (1), 52-56.

Peters, T. J., and Waterman, R. H., Jr. *In Search of Excellence: Lessons from America's Best Run Companies.* New York: Harper & Row, 1982.

Raudsepp, E. *How Creative Are You?* New York: Putnam, 1981.

Raudsepp, E., and Hough, G. P., Jr. *Creative Growth Games.* New York: Putnam, 1977.

Ray, S. *The Only Diet There Is.* Millbrae, Calif.: Celestial Arts, 1981.

Reddin, W. J. *Effective Management by Objectives.* New York: McGraw-Hill, 1971.

Rubin, I. M., and Berlew, D. E. "The Power Failure in Organizations." *Training and Development Journal,* 1984, *38* (1), 35-38.

Russell, P. *The Brain Book.* New York: Hawthorne Books, 1979.

Russell, W. F., and Branch, T. *Second Wind.* New York: Random House, 1979.

Satir, V. *Peoplemaking.* Palo Alto, Calif.: Science and Behavior Books, 1972.

Satir, V. *Making Contact.* Millbrae, Calif.: Celestial Arts, 1976.

Satir, V. *Your Many Faces.* Millbrae, Calif.: Celestial Arts, 1978.

Schein, E. H. *Organizational Culture and Leadership: A Dynamic View.* San Francisco: Jossey-Bass, 1985.

Schmidt, W. H., and Posner, B. Z. *Managerial Values and Expectations.* New York: AMACOM, 1982.

Schwarz, J. *The Path of Action.* New York: Dutton, 1977.

Schwarz, J. *Voluntary Controls.* New York: Dutton, 1978.

Scott, D. *How to Put More Time in Your Life.* New York: Rawson Wade, 1980.

Selye, H. *Stress Without Distress.* Philadelphia: Lippincott, 1974.

Shea, G. F. *Building Trust in the Workplace.* New York: American Management Associations, 1984.

Shealy, C. N. *90 Days to Self-Health.* New York: Dial Press, 1976.

Simonton, O. C., Matthews-Simonton, S., and Creighton, J. *Getting Well Again.* Los Angeles: Tarcher, 1978.

Smith, K. K. "Philosophical Problems in Thinking About Organizational Change." In P. S. Goodman and Associates, *Change in Organizations: New Perspectives on Theory, Research, and Practice.* San Francisco: Jossey-Bass, 1982.

Spice, M. B. "The Thought Selection Process: A Tool Worth Exploring." *Training and Development Journal,* 1982, *36* (5), 54-59.

Temple, S. *How to Meditate.* Chicago: Radial Press, 1971.

Thompson, J. "In Search of Excellence: A Conversation with Tom Peters." *Training and Development Journal,* 1983, *37* (8), 16-22.

Tjosvold, D. "The Dynamics of Positive Power." *Training and Development Journal,* 1984, *38* (6), 72-76.

Travis, J. W. *Wellness Workbook.* Mill Valley, Calif.: Wellness Resource Center, 1977.

Trubo, R. "How to Tap Your Brain's Success Circuits." *Success,* Mar. 1982.

Ulene, A. *Feeling Fine.* New York: Ballentine Books, 1977.

Ver Meulin, M. "When Employees Give Something Extra." *Parade Magazine,* Nov. 6, 1983, pp. 14-15.

Wagner, A. *The Transactional Manager.* Englewood Cliffs, N.J.: Prentice-Hall, 1981.

Wallis, C. "Stress: Can We Cope?" *Time,* 1983, *121* (23), 48-54.

Watson, C. E. *Results-Oriented Managing.* Reading, Mass.: Addison-Wesley, 1981.

Index